MODERN LEGAL STUDIES

IMMIGRATION LAW

AUSTRALIA
The Law Book Company Ltd.
Sydney : Melbourne : Brisbane

CANADA AND U.S.A.
The Carswell Company Ltd.
Agincourt, Ontario

INDIA
N.M. Tripathi Private Ltd.
Bombay

ISRAEL
Steimatzky's Agency Ltd.
Jerusalem : Tel Aviv : Haifa

MALAYSIA : SINGAPORE : BRUNEI
Malayan Law Journal (Pte.) Ltd.
Singapore

NEW ZEALAND
Sweet & Maxwell (N.Z.) Ltd.
Wellington

PAKISTAN
Pakistan Law House
Karachi

MODERN LEGAL STUDIES

IMMIGRATION LAW

by

J.M. EVANS,

B.A., B.C.L. (Oxon),

*Professor of Law, Osgoode Hall Law School,
York University, Toronto; formerly Lecturer
in Laws, London School of Economics*

LONDON
SWEET & MAXWELL
1976

Published in 1976 by
Sweet & Maxwell Ltd. of
11 New Fetter Lane, London.
Photoset by Red Lion Setters, London.
Printed in Great Britain by
Fletcher & Son Ltd., Norwich

ISBN Hardback 0 421 20230 0
Paperback 0 421 20240 8

PREFACE

I have attempted in this book to discuss immigration law and its administration in its historical and administrative context and to canvass some of the more important and often conflicting policies and considerations that have contributed to this rather curious and complex body of law. In addition, an attempt has also been made to relate the subject matter to some of the wider themes of English public law.

It would, of course, have been impossible to provide an exhaustive treatment of immigration law in a book of this size without sacrificing these wider aims. Whilst I am acutely aware that the book's omissions and emphases depend upon my only too fallible judgment, I selected for inclusion that amount of detail which seemed to me to illuminate some more general theme. Thus considerations of space explain the absence of any detailed account of, British nationality law, immigration in international law, extradition and the criminal offences created by the Immigration Act.

I am very grateful to the Editorial Board for their decision to include this work in the Modern Legal Studies Series and in particular to Professor W.R. Cornish for his encouragement and steadfastness. I am also grateful to the publishers for undertaking the preparation of the tables and index, and to my secretary, Miss Susan Kirk, for so resourcefully and cheerfully typing from a manuscript that would have caused others to despair.

Toronto,
July 1976

J.M. EVANS

OTHER BOOKS IN THE SERIES:

CONTENTS

TABLE OF CASES

TABLE OF STATUTES

Chapter 1

INTRODUCTION

British immigration law and its administration is a microcosm of many currently important issues of public law and government. This chapter first discusses some of the economic, social and political issues that have emerged during the turbulent history of immigration law since 1962. Some historical perspective is provided by the strikingly similar arguments that surrounded the first modern immigration legislation in this country, the Aliens Act 1905. Secondly, the chapter discusses some aspects of immigration law that relate to civil liberties and administrative justice. Its overall purpose is to examine the justifications for the regulation of immigration and to consider their implications.

Economic Purposes

As an aspect of economic policy immigration can be considered as a necessary evil for filling specific gaps in manpower, or as a general, dynamic force for economic expansion. The Aliens Act 1905 was seen by the Government of the day as having little to do with the impact of immigration upon the labour market.[1] The Act excluded aliens whose criminal record, medical condition or lack of actual or potential means to support themselves made them undesirable.[2] Although this legislation could be used to restrict the importation of contract labour at low cost (*e.g.* to break strikes) and to exclude labour for which there was already an overfull supply,[3] it was aimed primarily at excluding charges on public funds and not at protecting British labour. The protection of the home labour market, through the issue of work permits, has been an important factor in later legislation. The work permit scheme links immigration closely to immediate labour demand, for it normally allows a worker to enter for no more than 12 months to do a specific job with a named employer. When immigration control was extended to Commonwealth citizens in 1962 the regulation of the labour market was not the primary consideration; once admitted with an employment voucher, the immigrant was free to remain indefinitely and to choose his own job. During periods of severe labour shortage, especially in public service industries in big cities, government policy was still to restrict the number of employment vouchers issued.[4] The present position is that apart from EEC nationals whose entry may not be regulated by the level of labour demand, the general rule is that the work permit system applies to both aliens and Commonwealth citizens subject to immigration control.

Arguments about the economic impact of immigration, particularly of unskilled labour without capital, abound.[5] The protectionist case maintains that the availability of an almost inexhaustible fund of cheap immigrant labour provides a disincentive to employers to increase capital investment and productivity. Secondly, that the immigrants' demand for consumer and capital goods has an inflationary effect. Thirdly, that the increase in demand and cash remittances sent to dependants abroad adversely affect the balance of payments. Fourthly, that by increasing the unskilled labour available and thus keeping down the price of such labour, a redistribution of wealth is effected to the disadvantage of the lower paid workers with whom immigrant labour competes.

The free trade arguments emphasise that national wealth

must be increased by additions to the working force and that immigrants have introduced new industries and more efficient methods of production.[6] Secondly, that the immigration of workers represents a gift to the host community of the cost of their education and training. Thirdly, that immigrant labour tends to be more mobile and adaptable than resident labour. Fourthly, that since immigrant workers often move from a country where material expectations are lower, their demand for goods and social services is less than that of indigenous workers[7] and that since their percentage level of expenditure on consumption is less than the average,[8] the inflationary effects of immigration are highly marginal. In their study, Jones and Smith[9] showed that the unemployment rate for immigrants from the new Commonwealth (particularly the Caribbean and the Indian sub-continent) was only slightly higher than that for the population as a whole in times of economic expansion, but that during periods of recession the rate was significantly higher.[10]

Community Relations

The case for restricting immigration, especially from the "new Commonwealth," has, however, relied more heavily on the avoidance of conflict between the indigenous and immigrant populations and the creation of harmonious race relations. A similar rationale was advanced at the beginning of the century when the distinctive ethnic character of a substantial number of immigrants made immigration politically emotive.[11] Thus in 1905 during the debates on the Aliens Bill, the Home Secretary said:

> "One reason why I am anxious to get a settlement of this question of the regulation of the entrance of undesirables into this country is that I believe that if this grievance continues there is a chance in ignorant quarters of an anti-Semitic movement arising."[12]

Since the early 1960s "immigration," as an issue of public interest, has come almost exclusively to mean immigration by non-whites from the Caribbean, Africa and Asia. The following statement illustrates the race relations function assigned to immigration control:

"This policy has two aspects: one relating to control on the entry of immigrants so that it does not outrun Britain's capacity to absorb them: the other relating to positive measures designed to secure for the immigrants and their children their rightful place in our society, and to assist local authorities and other bodies in areas of high immigration in dealing with certain problems that have arisen."[13]

It is, however, very difficult to establish the truth of this crucial premise upon which government policies on immigration since the early 1960s have been based.[14] For good community relations depend not only upon the real impact of immigration upon the availability of employment, housing, education and social services, but also upon widely held perceptions of causal connections in such matters. But there is a good deal of authority that contradicts the basis of official policy. For example, Rose argues that the apparently unplanned changes in immigration policies after the 1962 Act, and their racially discriminatory effects, seriously undermined the confidence of the indigenous and immigrant population and consequently worsened race relations.[15] For the hasty passage of such legislation, apparently in response to popular hostility, whether real or politically inflamed, which has its greatest effect upon racial minorities, may reinforce the view of the majority that immigrants are indeed undesirable and increase the minority's sense of insecurity and suspicion. This has certainly been the view of the bodies with statutory responsibility for promoting good race relations.[16]

Even if it is conceded that immigration control can reduce tensions between the indigenous and immigrant, the content and administration of the legislation, as well as the prevailing political climate, will determine its success in achieving this objective. Whilst it is clear that throughout the 1960s the Government of the day was responding to political pressure from its back-bench supporters and from outside Parliament to restrict immigration by black and Asian people, the controls imposed were not in form racially discriminatory. Nonetheless, not only has their main impact been upon such people, but within the overall framework of control, special exceptions exist for citizens of Eire, nationals of other EEC countries and Commonwealth citizens with a grandparent born in the United Kingdom. In short, whilst denying that immigration control is racially discriminatory, governments have also acted upon the assumption that the nub of the problem has been the immigration of coloured people.[17]

Population Growth

A related, though distinct issue, is the place of immigration control in regulating the increase of population. Whilst, of course, it is impossible to predict the size of the immigration that would have taken place had restrictions not been imposed, Britain has typically been a country of net emigration[18] and the natural increase in the population is now only 0.04 per cent., the lowest for over 50 years.[19] If the effect upon population had been a primary matter of concern, then immigration control would have been imposed upon the freedom of movement between Eire and the United Kingdom.[20] The 1971 Census showed that just under 3 million people, comprising 5.5 per cent. of the total population, were born overseas, less than 40 per cent. (1.16 million) of whom were born in the new Commonwealth.

Although these figures demonstrate what a small contribution recent immigrants have made to the size of the total population, it has been argued that because of differences in colour and culture, the size of the "immigrant problem" can only be realistically appreciated by taking account of the children that will be born in this country of immigrant parents. At the 1971 Census it was estimated that about half a million children had been born in the United Kingdom of parents born in the Indian sub-continent or the Caribbean; it is also true that the birth-rate amongst women aged between 16-45 born in the new Commonwealth was in 1971 markedly above that for all women in the United Kingdom in this age range.[21] Another factor to which attention has been drawn is that the coloured population is concentrated in a relatively few areas and that this has a particularly disturbing effect upon the social patterns there.[22]

The essence of these arguments, associated particularly with Mr. Enoch Powell, is that the state may legitimately use immigration control to preserve the homogeneity of its population. But even before immigrants started arriving from the Caribbean in the 1950s in any appreciable numbers, the "homogeneity" of British society referred to was of colour, not culture, religion or ethnic or national origins. Of course, visible racial characteristics persist longer than cultural differences and discrimination on the ground of colour or race extends to children born here as well as to their overseas-born parents. In fact, the preservation of "racial homogeneity" has never been accepted by government as an objective of immigration policy. For not only does it have sinister overtones for all cultural and ethnic minorities, but in a multi-racial society is highly damaging to that very social cohesion which it claims to protect.

Housing and Social Services

A stronger case may be made for the use of immigration control to curb an already excessive demand for housing, education and social services, particularly when that demand is suddenly and unpredictably increased. The need to live where there is work and the desire for the support of compatriots already here, tend to concentrate immigrants into a few urban areas where social conditions may already be poor.

The Royal Commission of 1903 investigated the impact of immigration upon housing and found evidence that landlords were evicting their tenants in order to increase their profits by letting houses for multi-family occupation by immigrants. Their Report also noted an increase in the general level of rents in areas with the largest immigrant communities. Against this was to be balanced the fact that inadequate housing was not confined to those areas. The Report attached more significance to the effective enforcement of rigorous public health legislation than to immigration control as a means of mitigating the problem of overcrowding.

The housing shortage in urban areas has been urged as a reason for strict control of Commonwealth immigrants. But the study by Jones and Smith suggests that the principal impact of immigration upon housing, at a time when the shift of population from inner city areas to the suburbs was already taking place, has been to slow the pace at which old and inadequate housing and schools have been cleared to make way for new development,[23] although official policy now favours improvement rather than clearance.

Immigration law has not proved a very effective instrument for dealing with this aspect of policy.[24] For until the 1971 Act came into force it was British practice to impose control of Commonwealth citizens primarily at the port of entry. Whilst the work permit system could have been used to protect areas of the greatest housing shortage from further demands by alien workers, it does not appear to have been. However, during the passage of the 1971 Act, which extended the work permit system to Commonwealth citizens, the Government stressed the fact that the housing situation in the area of intended employment would be relevant to the issue of a work permit.

Before 1973 Commonwealth citizens had a virtually absolute right to immigrate as dependants of a United Kingdom resident, whereas alien dependants were admitted only if their sponsor provided adequate accommodation for them. The 1971 Act removed prospectively the statutory basis of the rights previously enjoyed by Commonwealth citizens and the new immigration rules apply the accommodation requirement irrespective of citizenship.

In short, the correlation between immigration policy and the supply of housing and the availability of educational facilities and social services has been fairly crude. Of much more direct relevance has been the allocation of special Exchequer grants to local authorities,[25] although the extent to which immigration policy increases the demands upon public revenue must be considered in assessing the overall economic impact of immigration. The high proportion of wage earners largely explains why the actual and projected cost per head of the social services, except education and child welfare, is lower for the Commonwealth immigrant population than for the total population.[26]

International Relations

Immigration law and policy may be used in the conduct of a state's relations with other countries. For example, a decision to admit or remove an individual may be influenced by the government's desire for good relations with the country of which he is a national. The overly prompt refusal to admit two Moroccan officers to Gibraltar in 1972, subsequently executed for attempting a coup against the Moroccan authorities, was presumably calculated to maintain good relations between the United Kingdom and Morocco. Similarly the legality of the removal of Dr. Soblen in 1963 from the United Kingdom to the United States of America where he had been convicted of espionage and of which he was a citizen, was upheld in the Court of Appeal on the ground, *inter alia* that the Home Secretary was entitled to consider the diplomatic and security consequences of surrendering the appellant whose return had been requested by the United States of America.

General immigration policy as well as individual decisions may also be significant in international relations. For example, the sweeping executive powers in the Aliens Restriction Act 1919 over former enemy aliens may have contributed to delaying the resumption of normal relations between the United Kingdom and Germany after the First World War. Recently, the relationship between immigration policy towards the admission of citizens of poor countries and the Government's programme of assistance to underdeveloped nations has been considered. On the one hand, there may well be circumstances in which a liberal immigration policy on the admission of workers may be of mutual benefit to the country of labour shortage and to the country where a reduction in the excess labour pool may significantly affect the rate of economic development. On the other hand, the pull of higher rewards available to the professional and highly skilled in the richer countries — the "brain drain" — may be detrimental to the countries of emigration. Although the economic significance of the movement of skilled labour is controversial,[27] the limitations imposed by the Government upon the number of doctors admitted to the United Kingdom, largely from the Indian sub-continent, may well have been influenced by these considerations.

International legal obligations may also restrict governmental freedom in the content of immigration policy. For example, membership of the EEC imposes an obligation upon the United Kingdom to ensure that it implements the free movement of labour provisions. It is a characteristic of EEC law that it can confer rights upon individuals that are enforceable in the national courts of Member States, as well as creating a legal relationship that gives rise to rights justiciable at the international level.

The United Kingdom's international obligations in respect of political refugees are now alluded to in the immigration rules, although the extent to which rights enforceable in the municipal courts have thereby been created is uncertain.[28] The United Kingdom has also been held in breach of the European Convention on Human Rights by the Commission insofar as its immigration law is racially discriminatory and infringes the right to family unity. The principal effect of a breach of international obligations is that the Government may decide that it is not prepared to pay the price of international opprobrium to maintain the impugned aspect of its policy. But recently, the appellate courts have used the Convention as an aid to an interpretation (favourable to the individual) of provisions of the Immigration Act 1971.[29]

Although the special position of Commonwealth citizens has been steadily eroded since 1962, so that in many respects they are treated on much the same basis as aliens, and less favourably than EEC nationals, a few vestiges of the special relationship between the United Kingdom and other Commonwealth countries remain in immigration law. In particular, a person possessing Commonwealth citizenship and an ancestral connection with the United Kingdom may be wholly or largely exempt from immigration control.[30] Civic and political rights within the United Kingdom extend to resident Commonwealth citizens, but not aliens.

Finally, the anomalous position of citizens of Eire, who although not Commonwealth citizens, have both remained largely exempt from immigration control and enjoyed the civic and political rights of British subjects, reflects the tortuous history of relations between the United Kingdom and Ireland.

Some Civil Liberties Issues

As with other restrictions imposed by the state upon personal freedom, legal powers that interfere with an individual's freedom to enter or remain in the country raise two issues. First, justification must be found for the substance of the power by striking an acceptable balance between the pursuit of a legitimate state interest and the interest of the individual in his freedom. Secondly, the form of the power should limit its exercise to the protection of legitimate state interests and provide as clear an indication of the scope as practicable; this latter point is closely connected with the questions of procedure and the appropriate means of reviewing its exercise.

It is not uncommon for states to afford fewer safeguards to the individual in immigration control than are normally required when an agency of the state deals with an individual in some other context. In the United Kingdom this is expressed in terms both of the absence of a legal right in the immigrant to enter or to remain beyond the period of the leave granted and of the range of considerations that the Executive may take into account in the exercise of a wide discretion.[31] Moreover, the traditionally very limited circumstances in which an exercise of prerogative power by the Crown in matters of foreign affairs and national security is reviewable also provide historical and constitutional explanations of the peripheral part played by the courts in regulating the relationship between government and individual in matters of immigration. Nonetheless, there has been in some respects a clear shift within the last 10 years towards more sharply delineating the circumstances in which discretion may properly be exercised; the importance of lawyers and legal values in the administration of immigration control and deportation has increased.

So far this chapter has emphasised the relationship between general immigration law and policy and other governmental objectives.[32] But even though an individual satisfies the criteria for admission or residence of a general category, he may be excluded or removed because he is personally unacceptable. Indeed the control imposed in the Aliens Act 1905 was primarily directed at the personal acceptability of the passenger. For it authorised exclusion if the officer was satisfied that the passenger was suffering from an illness or disability that endangered public funds or health, if he had a criminal record or lacked the means to support himself from present resources or future employment.[33] The legislation of 1914 and 1919, passed during periods of anxiety about possible threats to national security and political and industrial stability, posed by foreign spies and revolutionaries, widened the grounds of personal unacceptability to include those whose presence was deemed by the Home Secretary not to be conducive to the public good.

The width of the discretion, and the nature of the state interests at issue, have persuaded the courts that they have little part to play in reviewing the exercise of this power. Despite the gravity of the impact upon the individual, particularly when the decision adversely affects those who are established in the United Kingdom, the courts and governments have maintained that redress should be through the political process, not the judiciary. Even within the policy areas for which immigration powers are widely thought to be appropriately exercised against individuals, is it altogether clear why a foreigner who is established in the United Kingdom should be deported after conviction for even the most serious criminal offence, rather than be dealt with solely through the criminal process? Is it also beyond argument that the state may quite properly seek to advance its foreign policy by excluding an individual whose presence in the United Kingdom is a source of embarrassment to the government of another country? Even more dubious is the use of immigration power to exclude a person on the ground that his beliefs or the organisation to which he belongs, though not unlawful in any way, are considered by the Executive to be undesirable. The issue becomes most acute when the decision is calculated to discourage the lawful activities of individuals or organisations established in the United Kingdom, for example, trade unionists, political campaigns or religious movements, which cannot under existing law be directly restricted.

Some Administrative Aspects

Related to the purposes for which immigration powers may be exercised in individual decisions is the appropriate procedure at the stage of initial decision-making and the choice of the proper forms of review.

The choice of the appropriate procedure and of the proper forum and scope of review are related in large part to the nature of the power exercised. Thus in the absence of any express statutory guidance, the courts have not imposed procedural obligations upon the maker of a decision not to admit an alien or not to extend a leave to remain[34]; but they have appeared more favourably disposed towards requiring that the elements of procedural fairness — telling the individual the reason for the decision and allowing him an opportunity to reply — be observed before a person is deported.[35]

The more substantial the individual's interest that is adversely affected, the greater the need for procedural safeguards.

Although the 1971 Act contains powers of very considerable width to refuse entry and to deport, with the publication of immigration rules (which instruct immigration officers how to exercise their statutory discretion and provide guidance on the manner in which the Home Secretary will exercise his discretion after admission[36]), and the creation of appeal tribunals subject to the supervisory jurisdiction of the High Court, there is now a far closer scrutiny of Executive decisions by independent bodies. An important question remains about the types of decision that should be left to these tribunals rather than with the Home Secretary. The Act leaves with the Executive decisions that are made on grounds of national security, diplomatic relations or for reasons of a political nature. The argument is that tribunal expertise is unlikely to improve the quality of these decisions because they depend on situations that the Executive is best able to assess; that judicial-type proceedings are inappropriate where the Executive should not be required to disclose evidence upon which it relies, and lastly, the constitutional argument, that these decisions raise issues that may be closely related to areas of policy for which the government must accept ultimate responsibility. On the other hand, it is difficult to see why all decisions not to issue or to withdraw passports should be treated as raising non-justiciable issues, especially now that the Foreign Office publishes the grounds upon which it exercises the prerogative and since possession of a passport is a virtual necessity for the individual to travel abroad.

It is difficult to be sure whether this increase in judicialisation has made review through the political process less effective. One's impression is that less Parliamentary time is taken up by Members pressing the Home Secretary on individual cases.[37] Although the Home Secretary can always exercise a residual discretion to admit a person — thus remaining ultimately responsible for the decision — it is clearly relatively easy for him to defer any action until rights of appeal have been exhausted and then to say that to make a decision favourable to an individual in the teeth of a contrary decision from the tribunal, would undermine administrative consistency and the equal application of policy amongst people whose circumstances are materially similar. On the other hand, the work of the Parliamentary Commissioner for Administration and the Council on Tribunals,[38] the

statutory requirement that a statement of immigration rules
be laid before Parliament,[39] the establishment in 1968 of a
Select Committee on Race Relations and Immigration and the
high level of political interest in the subject have all tended to
increase the Parliamentary contribution to the formulation
and application of immigration law and policy.

Conclusion

Immigration law and administration provides a useful case
study of the difficulties inherent in balancing conflicting and
complex policies; that the law is in crucial respects based upon
a concept of nationality that is widely regarded as outmoded
— and which can only be effectively changed with the
co-operation of other governments — is an added
complication.

It is also worth noting two other aspects of the legislative
history on this subject. First, the pervasive consequences of
measures passed in haste to deal with a particular problem
that was seen at the time as requiring urgent attention. Thus
the Parliamentary deliberations on the 1914 Act occupy six
columns of Hansard, including a recital of its clauses! The
novel and sweeping Executive powers introduced in 1914 to
control the entry and removal of aliens were in substance
re-enacted in 1919, and that legislation was annually renewed
for over 50 years. The Commonwealth Immigrants Act 1968
was passed in three days; its principal feature, the submission
of certain United Kingdom passport holders to immigration
control, was embodied in the 1971 Act, the first
comprehensive and permanent legislation on immigration.

Secondly, there has been considerable governmental
ambivalence about much immigration legislation. There is
little doubt that in 1905, 1962 and 1968 Ministers reluctantly
introduced measures in large part responding to the activities
of vociferous pressure groups both outside and within
Parliament. But the governments were not prepared to

concede explicitly to the antipathy to the immigrant minorities that was widely expressed. Nor indeed did the legislation deal directly with the anxieties about, for example, employment, and housing that were partially responsible for the hostility to immigrants. Thus the 1905 Act was primarily justified by the need to exclude aliens with criminal records or who would be a charge on public funds.[40] Whilst the 1962 and 1968 Acts contained more effective machinery for controlling entry, no restrictions were imposed after entry that might have been relevant to alleviating the excessive demand for housing, educational facilities and the social services in particular areas. Moreover, the partial recognition by the government that it was legislating to defuse racial tension has enabled it to justify the special treatment given to Commonwealth citizens with an ancestral connection with the United Kingdom.

The danger, of course, is that compromises of this nature prove unsatisfactory. For they expose the law and its administration to a charge of hypocrisy; they feed, rather than assuage, the prejudices against immigrant groups; and they produce an unacceptably high degree of complexity and confusion in an area of the law and public administration where vital individual rights are at stake.

Notes

1 Although, Joseph Chamberlain enthusiastically supported the Bill on the ground that it afforded protection for British workers against foreign competition. He argued that protection was needed as much against foreign workers as against the goods that they produced.

2 s.1(3).

3 From 1906-13 the Appeal Board allowed 41 per cent. of the appeals made against exclusion on this ground. An explanation of this high figure is that it was common for prospective employers of immigrants to attend at the ports with offers of jobs.

4 A report published in October 1973 estimated that there was a manpower shortfall in London of 33 per cent. for council building workers,

20 per cent. for police officers, bus drivers and conductors, 14 per cent. for railway guards, station staff and tube train drivers and guards, and 11 per cent. for postmen and ambulance drivers: *The Sunday Times,* October 21, 1973.

5   See, for example, Jones, K. and Smith, A.D., *The Economic Impact of Commonwealth Immigration* (1970), *Economic Issues in Immigration* (Institute of Economic Affairs, 1970).

6   The Royal Commission on Alien Immigration of 1903 (Cd. 1741) did not find proved the allegation that immigrants, then largely Jews from Russia and Poland, had to any serious extent displaced resident labour in the areas of high immigrant concentration in east London (para. 131). Moreover, after 1895 the T.U.C. did not call for immigration control as a means of improving conditions of employment.

7   Jones and Smith at p.107 state that, "Taking all social security current expenditure and benefits together, the average immigrant received about 8o per cent. as much as the average member of the indigenous population in 1961 and the figure seems likely to be 85-90 per cent. by 1981." The study excludes from the definition of immigrant a child born in the United Kingdom to immigrant parents; although the unemployment rate amongst black school-leavers is now alarmingly high.

8   Figures for 1966 indicate about 8 per cent. difference: Jones and Smith, *supra*, at p.71.

9   *Supra.* See also Rose, *Colour and Citizenship* (1969) Chapter 31, where Professor Peston tentatively concludes that "on balance immigration has been economically beneficial to the economy, and I would add that excessive restraint on immigration might have adverse effects on the economy at large and on particular sectors." (p.655).

10 Thus in 1961 the unemployment rate amongst the immigrant group studied was 4.3 per cent. (compared with 1.6 per cent. for the total British-born labour force) and in 1966 1.63 per cent. compared with 1.37 per cent. (school leavers excluded from both groups). One explanation of the figures may be that new entrants to the labour market may have initial difficulties in securing employment and in times of recession may be laid off first.

The authors also conclude that the patterns of migration from the new Commonwealth specifically correspond, with a three month time-lag, to the availability of jobs in Britain, rather than generally to the higher standard of living (Chap. 2).

11 See Paul Foot, *Immigration and Race in British Politics* (1965); John A. Garrard, *The English and Immigration* (1971).

12 H.C. Deb. Vol.150, May 2, 1905, c.752.

13 *Immigration from the Commonwealth*, Cmnd. 2739 (1965), Introduction.

14 Foot (*supra*) argues that immigration policies have been based on the fallacy that prejudice is caused by immigrants, whereas the prejudice is in the indigenous population, fanned by unscrupulous politicians for their own purposes. But even so, the argument would be that strict control of immigration reduces fears upon which such prejudice appears to rest.

15 *Colour and Citizenship* (*supra*). See too Lester and Bindman, *Race and Law* (1972) who say, "in our view the effectiveness of the Race Relations Acts has been impaired by the tensions and contradictions between them and the immigration and nationality laws" (p.14).

16 The Community Relations Commission's Report for 1968-69 stated that the Commonwealth Immigrants Act 1968 "would make the task of promoting good community relations immeasurably more difficult" (para. 6). Its Report for 1971-72 stated that the Immigration Act 1971 "would adversely affect the establishment of harmonious community relations" (para.9) and the Report for 1972-73 concluded that the concessions made by the immigration rules in favour of Commonwealth citizens with a grandparent born in the U.K. "damaged the atmosphere in which we must work" (para.8).

The decision of the House of Lords in *Azam* v. *Secretary of State for the Home Department* [1973] 2 All E.R. 741 was regarded by the Chairmen of the Race Relations Board and of the Community Relations Commission as likely to damage race relations. (*The Times*, June 21, 1973.)

17 Leading articles in *The Times* have argued that Commonwealth immigration has only been restricted to curb the flow of coloured people and that restrictions on Australians, Canadians and New Zealanders are the "price we pay for hypocrisy." See issues for November 22, 1972, December 30, 1972. In *Racial Discrimination*, Cmnd. 6234 (1975) it is pointed out that immigration and race relations policies are now less interdependent. For in 1975 more than 40% of the coloured population of the U.K. was born here and with the sharp reduction in new immigration for settlement, the proportion will increase.

18 For example between 1964-73 emigration annually exceeded immigration by an approximate average of 61,000. An immigrant is defined for these purposes as a person who has resided outside the U.K. for the previous 12 months and who remains in the U.K. for the following 12 months; an emigrant is defined conversely. See *Ethnic Minorities in Britain* (C.R.C., 1974).

19 *Registrar General's Annual Estimates for 1973 and 1974.*

20 Although no immigration statistics are maintained, between 1967-71, 28,000 people from Eire registered each year for national insurance purposes. There is a significant turnover in the Irish population in the U.K.

21 The number of children born per 100 women born in the U.K. in 1971 was 8.2; the figure for women born in India and Pakistan was 19.8, 11.5 for women born in the West Indies and 11.4 for Eire-born women: *Registrar General's Second Quarterly Return for 1972.*

22 For example, in 1971, 476,000 people living in the Greater London area were born in the new Commonwealth (including Cyprus and Gibraltar), less than half the total of London residents who were born overseas: *GLC Research Memorandum 425* (1974).

23 *Supra*, Chap.7.

24 The Government refused to include in the 1905 Act a proposal of the Royal Commission that it should be a criminal offence, and a reason for deportation, for aliens to live in prohibited areas designated as such because of overcrowding. Compare the largely unsuccessful attempts of the Uganda Resettlement Board to keep refugees away from areas of high immigrant settlement and housing shortage: see Humphry and Ward, *Passports and Politics* (1974).

25 In 1973 60 per cent. of the urban aid programme (£16m.) went to areas with a substantial immigrant population, together with an extra £3m. to be spread over three years that would have gone as capital aid to Uganda. An Exchequer grant of 75 per cent. was also made in respect of expenses incurred by local authorities with substantial immigrant populations in the employment of staff under Local Government Act 1966, s.11. In the financial years 1970-73 the figure was £24m. (H.C. Deb. Vol. 855, May 3, 1973, c.1436 *et seq.*)

26 See Jones and Smith (*supra*) pp.100-107.

27 See, for example, Collard, "Immigration and Discrimination: Some Economic Aspects" in *Economic Issues in Immigration* (1970 I.E.A.). Remittances sent to relatives in the country of emigration may have an inflationary effect and be of little value in promoting economic development.

28 See below at pp. 67-69.

29 See *Waddington* v. *Miah* [1974] 2 All E.R. 377 (House of Lords used the presumption that Parliament did not intend to legislate in contravention of international obligations to construe s.34(1)(b) as not retrospectively imposing criminal liability. Had the U.K. ratified that provision of the Convention embodying the right of an individual to enter the country of which he is a national, the result of the Uganda Asian case, *Thakrar* v. *Secretary of State for the Home Department* [1974] Q.B. 684 might well have been different.

See also *R.* v. *Secretary of State for the Home Department ex p. Singh* [1975] 2 All. E.R. 1081 where Lord Denning affirmed the interpretative presumption and conceded that he had gone "too far" in *Birdi, The Times,* February 12, 1975, in suggesting that legislation in contravention of the Convention might be invalid. See also *R* v. *Secretary of State for Home Affairs ex p. Phansopkar* [1975] 3 W.L.R. 322 (C.A.).

30 See 1971 Act, s.2(1)(*d*), (2); H.C. 79, para.27, H.C. 80, para.25. The diminution in importance of the Commonwealth connection is also reflected in the recent immigration and citizenship legislation of Australia, Canada

and New Zealand, which have restricted the advantages previously given to British immigrants.

31 Wide powers of arrest, search and detention without trial are also considered necessary to the effective enforcement of immigration control: see 1971 Act, Sched. 2.

32 But in their application, general policies may greatly affect individual rights; for example, before 1974 there was no general right for a woman resident in the U.K. to be joined by her husband. The adverse effect upon the individual's family life must be weighed against the overall justification for general policies.

33 But the Act limited the definition of an "immigrant" to aliens, other than trans-migrants, travelling steerage class in a ship carrying more than a specified number of immigrants.

34 See *Schmidt* v. *Secretary of State for Home Affairs* [1969] 2 Ch. 149. But in *Re K.(H.)* [1967] 2 Q.B. 617 the Court held that a Commonwealth citizen seeking entry as of right under the 1962 Act as a child under 16 of a parent resident in the U.K. was entitled to a fair hearing.

35 See, for example, dicta in *Schmidt, supra*, at pp. 154, 156.

36 The curious legal status of this quasi-legislation is explored later.

37 This may, of course, be because the tribunals have eliminated injustices. This would seem, however, a rather overly optimistic view.

38 Whilst the Parliamentary Commissioner's jurisdiction to investigate complaints about decisions made by the staff of British High Commissions is limited, he has criticised the Home Office for failing to give adequate information to a person who wished to obtain an extension of leave to stay in this country (Second Report, 1968-69, H.C. 119, Case No. C845/68); for delaying the processing of an application for admission caused by an inadequate filing system (Second Report, 1971-72, H.C. 116, Case No. C467/5); and for a "human error" in removing an immigrant refused permission to land before the immigrant's solicitors had applied to have the decision quashed (Fourth Report, 1972-73, Case No. C531/9).

The Council on Tribunals was consulted on the procedural rules to be used by the appellate authorities: see also Annual Report of the Council on Tribunals for 1971-72 (1972-73, H.C. 13).

39 Immigration Act 1971, s.3(2). Indeed the Government was defeated in the House of Commons in December 1972 when it presented its statement and had to present a new statement to meet its critics. After its failure to carry a clause in the Bill exempting from immigration control Commonwealth citizens who have a grandparent born in the U.K., the Government successfully inserted the substance of this provision in the rules.

40 The 1919 legislation, with its provisions for dealing with former alien enemies of the Crown, in large part did reflect the contemporary political pressures.

Chapter 2

THE LEGAL BASES OF IMMIGRATION CONTROL

This chapter deals with the scope of immigration control by examining the definition of those who do not require the leave of an immigration officer to enter the United Kingdom.

Until 1962 British subjects had a common law right to enter the United Kingdom free from legal control and to remain for as long as they liked.[1] Since 1914 aliens have been statutorily required to seek leave to enter. There is also some authority for the existence of a common law power in the Crown to refuse entry to aliens.[2] Current legislation expressly preserves the Crown's prerogative powers, whatever they may be.[3] The scope of immigration control has thus rested principally upon nationality. Whilst any detailed discussion of British nationality legislation will not be pursued here, some explanation is necessary for an understanding of immigration law. For the reach of immigration controls has been, in different ways and at different times, related to the nationality status of the individual.

Nationality Law Background

The principal statute remains the British Nationality Act 1948[4] Its major innovation was to carve out of the old status of "British subject"[5] local citizenships to be acquired through a connection with a member of the Commonwealth. This change was made largely in response to the desire of the

Dominions for their own citizenship law; the former practice, under which uniform rules defined a British subject throughout the Commonwealth, was manifestly breaking down and producing anomalies. For example, under the Canadian Citizenship Act 1946, a child born outside Canada of a Canadian father did not take Canadian citizenship; yet under British law the child was a British subject. The scheme underlying the 1948 Act was to leave each independent member of the Commonwealth to define its own citizenship requirements and to provide that the normal way for acquiring the status of "British subject" was through citizenship of a member state of the Commonwealth. Whilst it was expected that a person who was a British subject in one country would be so regarded throughout the Commonwealth, it was recognised in 1948 that the rights attaching to that status would vary and that an independent member state might well not accord the same rights to all British subjects. Australia and Canada, for example, operated racially discriminatory immigration legislation at that time.

The British Government chose the United Kingdom and Colonies as the unit of citizenship under the 1948 Act, which also defines the methods of acquiring and losing that status. The arguments advanced in support of this decision were, first, that the geographical basis for citizenship should coincide with the area over which a single Parliament exercised legislative power; and secondly, that it recognised "the right of the colonial peoples to be regarded as men and brothers with the people of this country."[6] The Opposition's case, however, was that the Act artificially grouped together people who had less affinity with each other than that existing between people in Britain and the settlers of British origin in the Dominions.

Whilst it was acknowledged that all British subjects — irrespective of citizenship — enjoyed substantially the same rights under British law, an apprehension was expressed in the debates that in the future the rights of British subjects would tend to become linked to citizenship.[7] The principal cause of concern was that the Act diminished the importance of the common status of British subject by elevating the local citizenship as the means of acquiring the wider status. Another suggestion, of great topical interest,[8] was the creation of one citizenship of the United Kingdom and separate colonial citizenships.[9] The point was made by Lord Altrincham that a composite citizenship implied a

"... single geographical entity under one system of government, under which every member of the community has equal rights and responsibilities. But citizenship in that sense is obviously entirely inapplicable to a vast range of territories such as we have to deal with in the Colonial Empire and to an immense variety of peoples who range in the standard of civilisation and of civic responsibility from the head-hunters of Borneo to noble Lords opposite."[10]

The technical complexity of the 1948 Act was apparent enough at the time. Subsequent amendments, enacted in large part to accommodate the transition of Commonwealth countries from dependent to independent status and changing membership of the Commonwealth have produced a dauntingly formidable body of law. The basic amendment necessary to give legal effect to a change of citizenship status is an alteration to the list of countries in section 1(3). For the Act defines a Commonwealth citizen as a citizen of one of those countries.[11] Thus, provisions have commonly been made in legislation, enacted to give legal effect to a grant of independence, enabling certain categories of people to retain their status as citizens of the United Kingdom and Colonies until they become citizens of the newly independent state. Generally, these have been for the benefit of those with at least a grandpaternal connection with the United Kingdom or a colony.[12] The wider saving provisions were used for Kenya and Uganda, for example, because the Indian communities were apprehensive about their future in those countries.[13]

When South Africa and Pakistan left the Commonwealth legislation was passed, not only to make their citizens aliens, but also to make transitional provisions whereby for a limited period some could retain the rights of British subjects. The Pakistan Act 1973 eliminated Pakistan from section 1(3) of the British Nationality Act, but in the interests of the Pakistani community in this country made transitional provisions for the exercise of the rights of British subjects. For example, citizens of Pakistan who, on September 1, 1973, were in public employment from which aliens are normally excluded were allowed to retain their posts for another twelve months in which to decide whether to apply for registration as citizens of the United Kingdom and Colonies. Analogous extensions of the franchise and the right to acquire citizenship by registration rather than by naturalisation were also made.[14]

An anomaly of the 1948 Act that was manifest at the time was the provision made for citizens of the Republic of Ireland, which had left the Commonwealth in the previous year. The Government was faced with the task of balancing competing considerations. On the one hand, it was rightly felt that the majority of the population in the Republic wished not to be regarded, even by the Westminster Parliament, as British subjects. Further, the Irish Citizenship Act of 1935 provided that a person who became a citizen of another country would lose Irish nationality.[15] On the other hand, the migration between Ireland and the United Kingdom was regarded as mutually beneficial, there was a substantial Irish population in the United Kingdom at any given time enjoying full civic rights, and there were obvious practical difficulties of effectively enforcing immigration control. In addition, the claims of the "Southern Irish Loyalists" to remain British were strongly advanced in Parliament. The compromise embodied in the 1948 Act, with the agreement of the Dublin Government, was that whilst citizens of Eire were not British subjects, Eire not being a Commonwealth country listed in section 1(3), they were stated not to be aliens.[16] Thus citizens of the Republic of Ireland resident in the United Kingdom do not suffer the disabilities that attach to the status of alienage[17] and have been expressly included in the definition of those eligible to vote at municipal and parliamentary elections,[18] to serve on juries[19] and to hold public office.[20] The claims of the "Loyalists" were satisfied and the sensitivities of Dublin respected by a provision that persons who were British subjects immediately before the enactment of the 1948 Act could elect to remain so — not become — by writing to the Home Secretary stating that they had certain connections with the United Kingdom, by virtue of Crown service, possession of a United Kingdom passport issued in the United Kingdom or Colonies or "descent, residence or otherwise."[21]

The Commonwealth Immigrants Act 1962

This Act marked the first important step in the divorce of immigration rights from citizenship. Its most significant constitutional feature was that it fractured the immigration rights previously common to all British subjects. However, the concept of British nationality in its widest sense had already become greatly attenuated with the emergence of many newly independent Commonwealth states with widely differing political institutions, including republican constitutions, the growth in the populations of Canada and Australia of non-British origin and the increased attention being paid by the British Government to the EEC.

The political origin of the Act was a campaign mounted outside and within Parliament to restrict the entry of non-white British subjects.[22] A Bill was eventually introduced by the Conservative Home Secretary, Mr. R.A.

Butler, in very defensive and apologetic terms.[23] This, and subsequent measures, attempted to define the scope of control to meet the "mischief" as seen by its advocates without writing into the legislation overtly racially discriminatory provisions, whilst at the same time preserving as much "Commonwealth preference," both in terms of the scope and nature of the control, as was compatible with the other two aims.

The following table gives a picture of the numerical balance of migration in the years preceding the Commonwealth Immigrants Act 1962. Insofar as the argument for further control rested upon the dangers of overpopulation, the inward balance of migration for the four years before the Act was passed is, of course, striking — although the figures for 1958 are explicable largely by a decline in emigration to a more typical level. The big increase in the number of Commonwealth citizens immigrating in 1961 and the first half of 1962, especially from the Indian sub-continent, was almost certainly caused by the prospect of immigration control following the statement of Government intention announced at the Conservative Party's conference in that year.

The 1962 Act brought all British subjects, citizens of Ireland and British protected persons[24] under immigration control save for those who were born in the United Kingdom and those citizens of the United Kingdom and Colonies who held United Kingdom passports.[25] The scope of the control was justified by the Home Secretary on two grounds.[26] First that it exempted "persons who in common parlance belong to the United Kingdom." Secondly, that administration would be easy because the immigration officer need only look at the authority issuing the passport to tell whether the person was subject to control.

A United Kingdom passport was defined as one issued by the United Kingdom Government, and not one "issued on behalf of the Government of any part of the Commonwealth

Table
Immigration Figures pre-1962 Act

	1955	1956	1957	1958	1959	1960	1961	Jan.–June 1962
Net Immigration from Commonwealth	42,700	48,650	42,400	29,850	21,600	57,700	136,400	94,900
West Indies	27,550	29,800	23,000	15,000	16,400	49,650	66,300	31,800
India and Pakistan	7,350	7,650	11,800	10,900	3,800	8,400	48,850	44,130
Aliens admitted with work permits (and dependants)	41,080	45,393	42,029	42,443	41,345	47,166	51,365	
Less than 12 months	12,558	14,318	14,197	14,574	13,749	14,948	17,119	
Total National Insurance registration of the citizens of the Republic of Ireland		60,056	68,502	58,316	64,494	72,962	67,598	
Emigration from U.K.	101,050	220,000	230,000	142,000	130,000	124,000	123,500	
Balance of migration	−10,000	−17,000	−72,000	+45,000	+44,000	+82,000	+170,000	

Notes to Table

This table has been compiled from figures given in the annual reports of the Overseas Migration Board and the annual Statistics of Foreigners Entering and Leaving the United Kingdom.

1   The figures are very crude: they do not indicate the purpose or the length of the stay of the Commonwealth citizens, nor the ratio of workers to dependants. Later figures, however, indicate that the overwhelming majority of those coming from India and Pakistan were workers. No statistics were kept for immigrants from Australia, Canada, New Zealand, Rhodesia and South Africa.

2   The published figures for aliens show that they brought very few dependant children with them, but they do not indicate the length of stay. It has been estimated that the alien population permanently resident in the United Kingdom has annually increased by 15,000-20,000.

3   Because there were no immigration controls on the migration of citizens of the Republic of Ireland to and from the United Kingdom, these figures should be taken to include a substantial number of temporary and seasonal workers, and re-registrations by those returning to the United Kingdom. They do not include married women and children of school-age. From estimates made by the Registrar-General, the net immigration of citizens of the Republic of Ireland may be realistically set at about half of the total given for each year H.C. Deb. Vol. 715, July 5, 1965, c.177 (written answer).

4   In determining the overall migration figures, a migrant is defined as a person who moves his permanent place of residence for more than a year. The Overseas Migration Board, from its first report in 1954 (Cmd. 9261), deplored the inadequacy of the statistical information available to it. There were no reliable figures kept by a British Government

department for the movement of people by air transport and by the short sea routes between the United Kingdom and the Continent. The Board found the statistics kept by the governments of Commonwealth countries and the United States of their immigrants entering from the United Kingdom more reliable. The figures can do no more than indicate broad trends.

---

outside the United Kingdom.''[27] Passports issued by the Government of a colony[28] or by a British consulate in a foreign country[29] did not qualify their holders for exemption from immigration control. By exempting from control Commonwealth citizens born in the United Kingdom irrespective of their current citizenship and by extending immigration control to those whose citizenship of the United Kingdom and Colonies depended on a connection with a colony, the Act fulfilled a prophecy made in the debates on the British Nationalty Act 1948

> "We think that it is not likely, if any particular Parliament did feel minded to adopt discriminatory measures ... that it would proceed along the lines of division between the United Kingdom and Colonial citizens on the one hand and the citizens of other parts of the Commonwealth on the other hand.''[30]

Commonwealth Immigrants Act 1968

This Act extended the scope of control to those holders of United Kingdom passports not issued in the United Kingdom or the Republic of Ireland who could not also show that they had an ancestral connection with the United Kingdom by virtue of their or a parent's or grandparent's birth, naturalisation or adoption in the United Kingdom.[31] The constitutional significance of this measure was that it removed the legal right of entry from citizens of the United Kingdom and Colonies, even though they had no other citizenship and had no legal claim to remain where they were, because the territory from the connection with which their citizenship sprang had lost its colonial status.[32]

The immediate political background to this extraordinary piece of legislation, passed in three days in a Parliamentary atmosphere reminiscent of emergency measures passed under the shadow of war, was an increase in the flow of Asians from Kenya as the Kenyan Government introduced measures to restrict the trading activities of non-Kenyan citizens.[33] As a reuslt of the negotiations for Kenyan independence in 1963 it was provided that a person did not automatically become a citizen of Kenya on independence by virtue of his birth in Kenya if neither of his parents was born in Kenya. He retained his previous status of citizen of the United Kingdom and Colonies until he exercised the option of becoming a Kenyan citizen.[34] Many members of the Asian community decided not to opt for Kenyan citizenship after independence, fearing that discriminatory measures might be taken against them by the Kenyan Government's "Africanisation" policy.[35] The effect of the grant of independence to Kenya was to exempt those who retained their former citizenship from the operation of the 1962 Act. For their passports were now issued by the High Commission, on behalf of the United Kingdom Government, and not, as previously, on behalf of the Colonial Government. They thus became holders of United Kingdom passports as defined in the 1962 Act.

Whether this result was intended at the time of the independence negotiations was the subject of dispute amongst senior members of the Conservative Government that held office in 1963. Whilst any such intention was denied by the former Secretary for the Colonies and Commonwealth Relations, Mr. Sandys,[36] Mr. Maudling, in the debate on the 1968 Act said, "When [the Kenyan Asians] were given those rights it was our intention that they should be able to come to this country when they wanted to do so. We knew it at the time. They knew it and in many cases they have acted and taken decisions on this knowledge."[37] If the Asian community in Kenya were mistaken about the nature of the rights that they retained in 1963, it was a mistake shared by senior members of the Government with whom the Kenyan independence negotiations were conducted.

The arrangements made for the admission of such United Kingdom and Colonies citizens is discussed later, but it should be noted that the essential features of the extended scope of controls introduced in 1968 are restated in the current Immigration Act 1971. The position of those United Kingdom passport holders with no other citizenship and without a right of residence in a colony remains one of the most serious problems for the British Government in the areas of immigration law. It has been caused by the divorce of citizenship from exemption from immigration control. First, there is the humanitarian aspect involved in refusing entry to a passport holder who arrives in the United Kingdom without the additional documentation necessary to gain admission. [38] Return to the country of previous residence may be impossible or undesirable; there have been many instances of people being shuttled between airports or being temporarily accommodated in another country.[39] However, during the debate on the Bill, the Home Secretary acknowledged the limitation upon effective unilateral action by the British Government in this matter: "I was asked what we would do about a man who was thrown out of work and ejected from the country. We shall have to take him. We cannot do anything else in these circumstances."[40]

Secondly, grave doubts have been raised as to the propriety in international law of restrictions imposed upon the free entry into the United Kingdom of its citizens, especially when they had been expelled from the country where they were living. When United Kingdom passport holders and British protected persons were expelled from Uganda in 1972, the Government admitted them. Lord Chancellor Hailsham said of the position in international law that, "If a citizen of the United Kingdom is expelled from Uganda, and is not accepted for settlement elsewhere, we could be required by any state where he then was to accept him."[41] This issue was tangentially raised before the Court of Appeal in *Thakrar* v. *Secretary of State for the Home Department*,[42] where it was held that the provisions of the 1971 Act left no room for the operation of any rule of international law as part of British law to this effect. Lord Denning M.R. also doubted whether in any event such a rule applied to mass expulsions or to a country, like the United Kingdom, whose nationals were spread throughout the world. If the right existed it would, he said, be enforceable at the instance of another state and not by an individual.

He also doubted whether British protected persons, although issued with a passport, were British nationals in international law.[43] The British Nationality Act 1948 removed British protected persons from the scope of the statutory immigration controls over aliens,[44] without conferring upon them the status of British subject, from which many civic rights still derive.[45] Although they did not possess the common law rights of British subjects to enter and remain in the United Kingdom, they were in fact able to enter freely when in possession of a passport.[46] The position of British protected persons was also considered when Pakistan left the Commonwealth, for she passed a decree retrospectively making Azad Kashmiris citizens of Pakistan. They had previously been regarded as coming within the scope of the 1962 and 1968 Acts as British protected persons. Despite the argument initially put forward by the British Government that it was wrong that a country should be able, after leaving the Commonwealth, to confer upon people the status of

British subject, the provisions in the Pakistan Act were extended to Kashmiris. They thus enjoyed the benefits of the rights of British subjects for a transitional period after becoming aliens.

More recently, the European Commission on Human Rights found the British Government in breach of the European Convention by refusing to admit or to allow to remain, United Kingdom passport holders of Asian origin caught by the 1968 Act. The relevant articles, though not all may have been violated in each case heard by the Commission, were those dealing with protection from degrading treatment, protection of the right to family life and protection from discrimination on grounds of race, colour or national origin.[47] The Commission decided to refer the cases to the Committee of Ministers of the Council of Europe rather than the European Court of Human Rights, thus avoiding a definitive determination of the legal issues, and leaving them to political resolution.

The legal bases of exemption from immigration control contained in the Acts of 1962 and 1968 were built not only upon the statutory complexities of the British Nationality Acts but also upon the legal obscurities of the prerogative power to issue passports.[48] Despite the argument that by adopting possession of a United Kingdom passport as the principal legislative criterion for defining the scope of control, the administrative burdens would be eased,[49] legal difficulties nonetheless did appear. For example, in *Secretary of State for the Home Department* v. *Lakdawalla*[50] a refusal to remove the time restriction upon the leave to remain in the United Kingdom of a citizen of the United Kingdom and Colonies caught by the 1968 Act was attacked on the ground that the respondent was eligible to be issued with a United Kingdom passport in this country which would thus exempt her from control. The Tribunal held, however, that since the issue of a passport is within the absolute legal

discretion of the Crown, a person's eligibility to be issued
with a passport depended upon the rules currently applied by
the Foreign and Commonwealth Office. The Tribunal
accepted the evidence of an official that Passport Officers
had been instructed not to issue passports in the United
Kingdom to citizens of the United Kingdom and Colonies
who had not been admitted unconditionally and who fell
within the scope of the controls established by the 1962 and
1968 Acts. Thus, just as the ill-defined prerogative power of
the Crown in relation to aliens persists alongside the statutory
provisions,[51] so the operation of the statutory exemption
from control of some classes of British subjects depended
upon the exercise of the prerogative power over the issue of
passports.

The Immigration Act 1971

The current legislation has given the statutory framework of
immigration control a permanent basis. One of its aims was
to assimilate in a single code the immigration rights of British
subjects and aliens. It made two major changes in the legal
bases for exemption from immigration control. First, it
restores citizenship, rather than the type of passport as a
criterion for exemption. Secondly, it exempts from control
British subjects, irrespective of citizenship, one of whose
parents was born in the United Kingdom, whereas previously
the individual himself had to have been born here. A person
exempt from immigration control has a permanent right of
abode in the United Kingdom and is described in the Act as
being "patrial."[52] The following are the principal
categories who qualify for exemption.

(i)   *A citizen of the United Kingdom and Colonies* who
      (a) was born, adopted, registered or naturalised in the
      United Kingdom or Islands,[53] or
      (b) was born to or legally adopted by a parent who at

the time of the birth or adoption held citizenship of the United Kingdom and Colonies by one of the ways specified above, or

(c)   had a grandparent who satisfied the same criteria, [53] or

(d)   has at any time been settled in the United Kingdom and Islands and had at that time been ordinarily resident there for the last five years,[54] or

(e)   being a woman has been at any time married to a man who qualified within (a) (b) or (c).[55]

(ii)   *A Commonwealth citizen* who

(a)   has one parent who was born in the United Kingdom or Islands and who was a citizen of the United Kingdom and Colonies at the time of the birth of the *praepositus*, [56]

(b)   being a woman has been married to a person who qualifies within (i) or (ii)(a) above.[55]

Detailed discussion of these provisions can be found elsewhere,[57] but some points of wider significance need to be mentioned. First, the Act exempts from control an unquantified number of people who do not hold United Kingdom passports but who are dual citizens of the United Kingdom and Colonies and of another country. For example, a person born abroad who has not renounced his citizenship will be patrial if at the time of his birth his father was a United Kingdom and Colonies citizen by birth. Citizenship by descent can generally be extended beyond the first generation only by registration[58]; but the registration of children of citizens of the United Kingdom and Colonies by British High Commissioners after the passing of the 1971 Act will not qualify as "registration in the United Kingdom."[59] Secondly, an estimated five million people are exempt from control under section 2(1) (*d*); this provision partially compensates for the fact that a married woman does not confer her citizenship upon her child under the British Nationality Acts. For example, a child born in Canada of a Canadian father and a United Kingdom-born mother who has retained her citizenship will be patrial, whilst another child born in the United States of an American father and a United Kingdom-born mother will not. Thirdly, the exemption from control based upon citizenship and residence in the United Kingdom is likely to produce difficult problems because of the complexity of the statutory definitions. In particular, a person is only "settled" when there are no restrictions on his leave and he is ordinarily resident without being here in breach of the immigration laws.[60]

The broad justification advanced for the patriality provisions of the 1971 Act is that they reflect notions widely accepted throughout the community of who "belongs" to the United Kingdom. In a post-Imperial era it is not surprising that those whose citizenship depends upon a connection with a colony are not regarded as "belongers." Nationality supported by ancestral connection (with citizens of the United Kingdom and Colonies who come within section 2(1)(b) having the advantage of a connection two generations removed), and citizenship linked with a period of unrestricted residence in the United Kingdom are the bases for exemption.

Whether this justification is sound is dubious. To have taken the scheme of the British Nationality Act 1948, passed at a time when the idea of Empire and of Britain's place as the "home country" had wide currency, as the starting point for immigration classification in 1971, was indeed curious. Should an immigrant to Australia or Canada who acquires local citizenship be exempt from immigration control whilst an emigrant to the United States who becomes a citizen is not? Should the Canadian-born child of a woman who retains United Kingdom citizenship after her marriage to a Canadian be exempted from control when he would not be if the non-United Kingdom factors had been American rather than Canadian? The restrictions of the 1948 Act upon the transmissibility of citizenship through women also seem out of line with contemporary notions of sexual equality before the law. These restrictions may, of course, be quite unrelated to the existence or strength of family ties with relations still living in the United Kingdom. The change of status that can be effected by operation of law, for example, when a former colony acquires independence or a member state leave the Commonwealth, also emphasises the artificiality of the concept of patriality.

The most serious criticism made of British immigration law is that it is racially discriminatory, and that this is apparent in the very definition of the scope of immigration control. The principal arguments used to refute this charge are that the terms of the legislation do not expressly discriminate on grounds of race or colour, that the scope of exemptions from control are based on family connections with the United Kingdom and that the reason why most of those who benefit are white is because until fairly recently the United Kingdom has not been a multi-racial society. It is, of course, true that the legislation is not in terms racially discriminatory, that many patrials by virtue of their citizenship and residence in this country will be black, and that many white Commonwealth citizens are not patrial because their ancestral connection with the United Kingdom is not sufficiently close. Nonetheless, attitudes to racialist pressure have been equivocal, as the following statements made during the debates on the 1968 Act show:

"I think that in discussing this Measure we must not be in any way hypocritical about the racial nature of the problem that underlies it."
"It has been argued that [clause 1] is racial in intent. I do not think that this is so."[61]

It is impossible to believe that immigration control would have been extended to cover United Kingdom passport holders had the refugees from East Africa been of British descent. In this sense, at least, the legislative classifications are racially inspired. Moreover, insofar as patriality reflects links with the United Kingdom through family, it works one way. It favours the descendants of emigrants, but not the families of recent immigrants. A definition of "belonging" that excludes citizens who have no legal claim to remain in any other territory, but includes some British subjects who are not citizens of the United Kingdom and Colonies would seem to be open to a strong suspicion of racial discrimination.

Whilst many of the complexities and inelegancies of the current law may be remedied by the passage of a new United Kingdom Citizenship Act which will re-align citizenship and exemption from immigration control, it is unlikely that it will effect major changes in the practical operation of the present law. The crucial issue will be the provisions made for those whose present citizenship of the United Kingdom and Colonies derives from their connection with a former colony. But it is not within the power of the United Kingdom Government to deal with the problem satisfactorily without the co-operation of other interested states.[62]

Notes

1 See *D.P.P.* v. *Bhagwan* [1972] A.C. 60.

2 The principal case is *Musgrove* v. *Chun Teeong Toy* [1891] A.C. 272. Despite the criticisms made of this and other decisions by Thornberry in 12 *I.C.L.Q.* 414, 422-428, it appears to be now widely accepted; see *Schmidt* v. *Home Office* [1969] 2 Ch. 149, where Lord Denning M.R. said, "...at common law no alien has any right to enter this country except by leave of the Crown." Widgery L.J. (at p.155) took a similar view.

3 Immigration Act 1971, s.33(5).

4 Amending legislation has subsequently been passed; for a complete list see Halsbury, Vol.4, *British Nationality*, p.401 (3rd ed. 1974).

5 A common law concept based upon allegiance to the monarch.

6   H.C. Deb. Vol. 453, July 7, 1948, c.394 (Mr. Chuter Ede).

7   "If we create a special citizenship, then it will require a more than usually sustained fight to prevent someone at some stage attaching some meaning to that citizenship by giving it special rights and privileges and that is the danger which I envisage." H.C. Deb. Vol. 454, July 19, 1948, c.67 (Sir D. Maxwell Fyfe).

8   Work along these lines has been in progress since early 1973 and in 1975 Mr. Alex Lyon, Minister of State at the Home Office announced the Government's intention to introduce new citizenship legislation before the end of the life of the present Parliament: *The Sunday Times*, May 6, 1975.

9   See H.C. Deb. Vol. 453, July 7, 1948, c.1095.

10   H.L. Deb. Vol. 156, June 21, 1948, cc.995-996.

11   s.1(1). The terms "Commonwealth citizen" and "British subject" are interchangeable (s.1(2)), although the Act provides for a class of British subjects who have no local citizenship (see ss.13(1), 16). When a country is added to s.1(3) persons whose citizenship of the U.K. and Colonies had depended solely on their connection with that colony automatically lose their previous citizenship. For the Act defines "Colony" as not including any country so listed (s.32(1)). See, for example, Grenada Independence Act 1973. The Bangladesh Act 1973 added a new country to the s.1(3) list.

12   See Halsbury, Vol. 4, *British Nationality*, pp.445-447.

13   Kenya Independence Order 1963, S.I. 1963, No. 1968 art. 1(1) provided that a person shall not become a citizen of Kenya if neither of his parents were born in Kenya. Art. 2(1) entitled such persons to register as Kenya citizens if they would otherwise have become Kenyan citizens on independence. A survey made in 1968 estimated that 40-50,000 Asians automatically became Kenyan citizens, 20,000 had opted for Kenyan citizenship, and that about 100,000 Asians had retained their previous status — either as citizens of the United Kingdom and Colonies or as a British protected person. See, David Steel, *No Entry* (1969). Analogous provisions are contained in Uganda Independence Order 1962, S.I. 1962, No. 2175, Arts. 7, 8.

14   See, especially, s.3 and Sched. 2. The Pakistan Act 1974 amends s.3(5) and extends the registration period. By February 1975, 103,000 applications for citizenship had been made.

The corresponding provisions of the South Africa Act 1962 were substantially more generous, allowing citizens of the Republic to continue in employment from which aliens are barred until the end of 1965; a person could give notification of intention to register as a citizen of the United Kingdom and Colonies up to that date: s.1, Sched.1.

15   In *Murray* v. *Parkes* [1942] 2 K.B. 123 the Divisional Court held that a person born in Ireland in 1908, but who had long resided in England, was

liable to conscription as a British subject. The Court found no Act of the Westminster Parliament that had deprived such people of their status as British subjects by birth in the U.K. or one of the Crown's dominions and rejected the argument that "a British subject can be deprived of that status by Act of some Government, State or Dominion elsewhere" (at p.136 per Singleton J.).

16 B.N.Act, s.32(1). The Ireland Act 1949, ss.1, 2, formally recognised that the Republic of Ireland was no longer a Dominion but provided that it was not a foreign country.

17 For these see Halsbury, Vol. 4, *Aliens*, pp.465-469.

18 Representation of the People Act 1949, ss.1(1), 2(1). British Nationality Act 1948, s.31, Sched. 4 repealed the provision in the Act of Settlement 1700 insofar as it disqualified British subjects and Irish citizens from membership of the Privy Council and both Houses of Parliament and offices under the Crown.

19 The criteria for eligibility are the franchise and five years' ordinary residence in the U.K. since the age of 13: Criminal Justice Act 1972, s.25.

20 British Nationality Act 1948, Sched.4 (*supra* n.18.).

21 s.2. The declaration was enough; it was not necessary to satisfy the Home Secretary that any of the stated connecting factors actually existed. The benefit of this provision does not apply to anyone born after the 1948 Act came into force and the status of British subject acquired under s.2 is not transmissible.

22 For the political background, see Paul Foot, *Immigration and Race in British Politics* (1965).

23 See H.C.Deb., Vol. 649, November 16, 1961, c.687 *et seg*.

24 These were people connected with territories that were never Crown colonies but were administered, for example, through local rulers or under international mandate (*e.g.* Uganda and Tanganyika). Until the British Nationality Act 1948 they were regarded as aliens, but the 1948 Act declared them not to be aliens without making them British subjects. They did not enjoy those civic rights which depended on the status of British subjecthood (*e.g.* the franchise) but were not subject to the statutory immigration controls over aliens. *Quarere*, whether the Crown's prerogative is limited to aliens or does not extend to British subjects.

25 s.1.

26 H.C.Deb., Vol. 649, November 16, 1961, c.695.

27 s.1(3).

28 *R.* v. *Secretary of State ex p. Bhurosah* [1968] 1 Q.B. 266.

29 *Mamacos* v. *Secretary of State* [1972] Imm.A.R. 11.

30 H.C. Deb., Vol.454, July 19, 1948, c.50 (Sir Hartley Shawcross, Attorney-General).

31. s.1, which became s.1(2A) of the 1962 Act.

32 The International Commission of Jurists estimated in 1968 that 350,000 people who had no other citizenship then came under the Act's control. In 1973 the Government estimated the number at 240,000: H.C. Deb., Vol. 851, February 22, 1973, c.139 (written answers). During the passing of the Bill, Lord Gardiner estimated that 2.4 million citizens of the U.K. and Colonies were exempt from the 1962 Act but would fall within the proposed measure. (H.L. Deb. Vol. 289, February 29, 1968, c.924-925). More recently, it has been estimated that there are 45,000 U.K. passport-holders with no other citizenship in East Africa: H.C. Deb. Vol. 899, Nov. 12, 1975, c.766 (written answer).

33 Separate figures for U.K. passport holders coming from East Africa appear to have been kept from 1965. The relevant stastics of immigrants with U.K. passports from East Africa were 6,149 in 1965, 6,489 in 1966, 13,600 in 1967. On the basis of the figures for the latter part of 1967, the Government projected an inflow of 20,000 for 1968. But as before the 1962 Act was passed, the numbers may have been swollen by attempts to avoid the impending control.

34 1963 S.I. 1968, s.1(1). On the other hand, the Kenya Independence Act 1963 s.3(2) provides that a person shall not cease to be a citizen of the U.K. and Colonies even if he became a Kenyan citizen on independence if he or his father or grandfather was born in the U.K.

35 See generally David Steel, *No Entry*, where it is estimated that on the basis of an Asian population in Kenya of 170,000 in 1962, 40-50,000 automatically became Kenyan citizens on independence and that another 20,000 opted for Kenyan citizenship.

36 H.C. Deb. Vol. 759 February 27, 1968, c.1276.

37 *Ibid.* at c.1345. He nonetheless concluded that the Bill was justified because of the likely harm to community relations in this country that would be caused by "the arrival in this country of many people of wholly alien cultures, habits and outlook" (*ibid.*). It was also the view of the Labour Government that introduced the 1968 Bill that it derogated from the assurances given in 1963 (see especially, the speech by Mr. David Ennals, Under Secretary of State at the Home Office, *ibid.* c.1354).

38 Because they may be required to remove a person at their own expense who has been refused admission, carriers attempt to ensure that their passengers have the documents required by immigration authorities. In the early hours of Friday March 1, 1968, in the last stages of the Lords' debate, it was alleged in the House that BOAC was already refusing to carry Asians who fell within the new controls.

39 For example, between March 1, 1968 and January 31, 1970, 42 U.K. passport holders were refused entry. In July 1972, of the U.K. passport holders refused entry 99 were detained in the U.K., 56 in Italy, 21 in France and 2 in Spain. (H.L. Deb. Vol. 333 July 19, 1972, c.761.).

40 H.C. Deb. Vol. 759 February 27, 1968, c.1501.

41 H.L. Deb. Vol. 335, September 14, 1973, c.497. But in a statement made earlier that year the Home Secretary, Mr. Robert Carr, cast doubt upon the Government's willingness to honour its obligations to U.K. passport holders in the event of another mass expulsion, because it would "impose unacceptable strains and stresses on our society": H.C. Deb. Vol. 846, c.654-656.

42 [1974] 2 All E.R. 261.

43 For a fuller discussion of the international law aspects of the problem, see Richard Plender, *International Migration Law* (1972), pp.88-93.

44 s.3(3). s.32(1) provides that for the purposes of the Act "alien" does not include a British protected person. See generally, Clive Parry, *Nationality and Citizenship Laws*, Vol.I, Chap. 7. However, like aliens, they acquire citizenship by naturalisation at the discretion of the Secretary of State, whereas before the Immigration Act 1971, British subjects acquired it as of right by registration.

45 Whilst the British Nationality Act 1948 s.31 amended the Act of Settlement 1700 so as to enable British subjects, wherever born, to sit in Parliament, British protected persons remain ineligible. The franchise, for Parliamentary and local elections, is limited to British subjects and citizens of Eire: Representation of the People Act 1949 ss.1(1), 2(1)(*b*). Eligibility for jury service depends upon registration as an elector: Criminal Justice Act 1972, ss.25, 26. The British Nationality Act also left unrepealed the definition of aliens in the Status of Aliens Act 1914, s.27, which includes anyone who is not a British subject. s.17 of this Act imposes certain restrictions upon the ownership of property by aliens and disqualifies them from office. See also Local Government Act 1972, S.79. The Aliens Employment Act 1955, s.1(1)(*b*) on the other hand, exempts British protected persons from the statutory disabilities of aliens for employment under the Crown.

46 An amendment made in 1943 to the Aliens Order 1920, article 22(1A) provided that aliens who were British protected persons were to be deemed not to be aliens for the purposes of the Order. See too, Aliens Order 1953, article 24(2). The British Nationality Act definition of "aliens" is used in Immigration (Registration with the Police) Regulations 1972, S.I. 1972 No. 1758 and Immigration (Hotel Records) Order 1972, S.I. 1972 No. 1689.

47 *The Times*, May 29 and June 5, 1974. The British Government has not ratified the Fourth Protocol of the Convention which unequivocally provides that "no-one shall be denied the right to enter the territory of which he is a national."

48 See JUSTICE Report, *Going Abroad; A Report on Passports* (1975), noted in (1975) 38 M.L.R. 314.

49 On the extension of controls in 1968, passports issued by British High Commissions were stamped to show whether the holder was free from

immigration control. (761 H.C. March 26, 1968, c.342).

50 [1972] Imm.A.R. 26.

51 Immigration Act 1971, s.33(5).

52 ss.1(1), 2(6).

53 s.2(1)(*b*)

54 s2(1)(*c*).

55 s.2(2).

56 s.2(1)(*d*).

57 *Halsbury's Laws of England*, Vol.4, paras. 901 *et seq.*; I. Macdonald, *The New Immigration Law* (1972).

58 British Nationality Act 1948, ss.5, 8.

59 s.2(4). See also s.2(2) which excludes from the class of citizens of the U.K. and Colonies by registration, women who registered after the Act by virtue of marriage to a citizen of the U.K. and Colonies after the Act. This limitation was inserted primarily in order to prevent the wives of non-patrials indirectly acquiring patriality as a result of their marriage. As part of the Act's policy to assimilate the position of aliens and "non-belonging" Commonwealth citizens, an important amendment was made to the British Nationality Act 1948; the registration of British subjects or citizens by virtue of residence in the U.K. is now within the discretion of the Secretary of State. It was previously automatic after five years' residence. Apart from some transitional provisions, the rules relating to registration and naturalisation are now very similar. See Sched. 1. It is unlikely that discretion will be exercised in favour of a Commonwealth citizen whilst his leave to remain is restricted. Naturalisation by the Governor of a Protectorate does not qualify for patriality: *Keshwani* [1975] Imm. A.R.38.

60 ss.2(3)(*d*), 33(2). See *Azam* v. *Secretary of State* [1973] 2 All E.R. 765. Whilst the immediate effect of this decision, *viz.* the retrospective liability of persons who illegally entered before the 1971 Act was passed to be removed as illegal immigrants, has been muted by the amnesty announced in 1974, the House of Lords' interpretation of this phrase has applicability in several provisions of the Act. For example, s.1(5) (returning Commonwealth citizens previously settled in the U.K.: see *ex p. Mughal* [1973] 3 All E.R. 796), s.2(1)(*c*) (patriality depends upon being settled), s.7(1) (limitation upon liability for deportation of Commonwealth citizens ordinarily resident in the U.K. before January 1, 1973).

61 H.C. Deb. Vol. 759, February 28., 1968, c.1345-1346 (Mr. Maudling).

62 In *Racial Discrimination*, Cmnd. 6234 (1975) it is conceded that the lack of a clear-cut definition of citizenship and the regulation of immigration through manipulating the concept of nationality have given a racially discriminatory cast to immigration legislation.

Chapter 3

SOME SPECIAL CASES

Superimposed upon the general principles regulating entry
into the United Kingdom discussed in the next chapter, the
Act and the rules make special provision for the admission of
some non-patrials. The exceptions to the overall philosophy
of immigration control, in favour of those with "vested
rights" when the Act came into force, Commonwealth
citizens and those travelling within the common travel area,
are the result of balancing competing policies. Conversely,
the Prevention of Terrorism (Temporary Provisions) Act
1974 empowers the Home Secretary to exclude patrials from
the United Kingdom,[1] and it is certainly very arguable that a
patrial who should have had a certificate of patriality may be
excluded in its absence.[2]

Commonwealth Citizens

As we have seen, Commonwealth citizenship is one of the
essential requirements of patriality. It is also necessary for the
enjoyment of many important civic rights. Additionally,
immigration law confers benefits upon some Commonwealth
citizens who are not patrial, thus qualifying one of the basic
purposes of the 1971 Act, namely, the assimilation of the
rights under immigration law of non-patrial British subjects
and aliens.

   (a)   The 1971 Act preserves the existing statutory rights of
entry of returning residents and of the wives and children of

those already in the United Kingdom[3] by providing in section 1(5) that the immigration rules shall not be framed so as to render Commonwealth citizens settled in the United Kingdom on the day that the Act comes into effect and their wives and children "any less free to come into or go from the United Kingdom than if the Act had not been passed." The burden of proof is on the individual.[4]

The first qualification to note is that to come within the section a person must be settled, *i.e.* he must be ordinarily resident without being here in breach of the immigration laws and not subject to any restriction on his leave to remain. In *R.* v. *Secretary of State for the Home Department ex parte Mughal*[5] the applicant, a citizen of Pakistan, had been refused entry as a returning resident. In dismissing the application for *habeas corpus* Scarman L.J. said:

> "The effect of [s.1(5)] (to which the immigration rules faithfully adhere) is that any such citizen who satisfies an immigration officer that he is ordinarily resident in the United Kingdom, or had been so at any time during the two years preceding his entry, is to be allowed to enter. The ordinary residence to which the section refers is, of course, lawful residence: see *Re Abdul Manan*."[6]

After the House of Lords' decision in *Azam*,[7] it would seem that a person who originally landed in the United Kingdom without obtaining leave, after this had been made a criminal offence under the 1968 Act, cannot claim the benefit of section 1(5) because he will be unable to show that he was lawfully resident in the United Kingdom when the 1971 Act came into force. Whether this reduces the right of re-entry that existed under the 1962 and 1968 Acts is unclear; in *Re Abdul Manan*[8] the applicant had entered after deserting his ship, thus committing a continuing offence and remaining liable, without any time limit, to removal. Indeed, this was Lord Denning's primary justification for interpreting the Act to mean lawfully ordinarily resident. On the other hand, it has been held that residence for five months following an unconditional entry is sufficient to establish that the immigrant is ordinarily resident for the purpose of exercising a right to re-enter.[9]

Under the 1962 Act a "wife" includes a partner to a polygamous marriage valid by the law of the parties' domicile.[10] In a surprising recent decision the Immigration Appeal Tribunal has held that section 1(5) applied to the Pakistani wife of a Commonwealth citizen settled in this country, who was seeking entry after she had become an alien under the Pakistan Act 1973.[11] Whilst it is true that section 2(2)(*b*) of the 1962 Act did not expressly state that the wife must be a Commonwealth citizen, section 1(1) stated that the Act shall control the immigration of Commonwealth citizens, other than those exempted by virtue of their connection with the United Kingdom by birth or ancestry. The most important practical consequence of treating a wife as within section 1(5) is that her right of entry, unlike that of others, does not depend upon her husband's ability and willingness to support her.[12] In *Bee*, the wife would not otherwise have been admissible since her husband was then in prison.

The scope of the statutorily protected right of children of Commonwealth citizens settled in the United Kingdom on January 1, 1973 is limited to children under the age of 16. It excludes the child one of whose parents (including the natural or putative parents of an illegitimate child) is neither settled in the United Kingdom nor seeking entry. This restriction, imposed by the 1968 Act, was designed to restrict the entry of children likely to give rise to social problems. In particular, the children of unsupported mothers (especially from the West Indies) and male children just under school leaving age joining all male households (a not uncommon feature of early immigration from Pakistan and India).[13]

(b) Although the Government was defeated on its

proposal to include within the definition of patrials Commonwealth citizens with a grandparent with United Kingdom and Colonies citizenship acquired by birth in the United Kingdom, the immigration rules give substantial advantages to Commonwealth citizens with a United Kingdom-born grandparent. Thus they are admissible for an indefinite period if they have an entry certificate, to be issued on satisfactory proof of the relevant ancestral connection.[14] This is an important qualification to the general legislative policy against first-time settlement from the date of entry.

Whilst several million people are entitled to these concessions, most of whom are citizens of Australia, Canada and New Zealand, it is unlikely that more than a few will claim them. The concessions were introduced after the Government's defeat on its first set of rules under the 1971 Act as a result of an alliance between the Opposition and some Conservative backbenchers who felt it wrong that "old Commonwealth" citizens should be treated less favourably than EEC nationals. The exemptions have been strongly criticised. First because they are compatible with only a tenuous connection with the United Kingdom[15] that does not justify such favourable treatment when strict control is exercised over other immigrants, in particular some United Kingdom passport holders and dependants of Commonwealth citizens resident in the United Kingdom. Secondly, they appear to give immigration advantages to non-citizens on the basis of racial and ethnic origins and as such are detrimental to the development of good race relations in this country. At a time when strict control is exercised over the entry of non-patrial United Kingdom and Colonies citizens and dependants of Commonwealth citizens resident in the United Kingdom the exceptions show, at the very least, a lack of sensitivity.[16] Thirdly, they are unnecessarily divisive in their operation amongst citizens of differing ethnic origins in the Commonwealth countries most likely to be affected,

Australia, New Zealand and Canada.[17]

(c) The immigration rules also entitle young Commonwealth citizens to enter for a period of 12 months, with extensions of up to five years, as "working holiday-makers." [18] This is a partial exception from the work permit rules in favour of Commonwealth citizens. The employment must be "incidental to their holiday."[19] About 15,000 people, mostly from the "old" Commonwealth countries, take advantage of this scheme each year.

(d) Other advantages conferred upon Commonwealth citizens by the immigration rules are their exemption from liability to register with the police[20] and an apparently more flexible attitude towards their remaining as trainees.[21]

Miscellaneous

(a) A transitional provision of general application is contained in section 1(2) whereby non-patrials who were in the United Kingdom and settled when the Act came into force are treated as having indefinite leave to enter or remain in the United Kingdom. Its scope, however, is more limited than might at first appear. For in *R.* v. *Secretary of State ex p. Mughal*[22] the Court of Appeal held that its operation was confined to those ordinarily and lawfully resident within the *Azam* rule and that it is also necessary for the immigrant to prove that he was physically present in the United Kingdom on January 1, 1973. Secondly, despite the reference to indefinite leave to enter or remain, the section does not confer any automatic right of re-entry. For section 3(4) provides that all leaves lapse when a person travels outside the common travel area[23]; under section 3(8) the onus of proof is on the immigrant to establish, for example, that he is entitled to admission as a returning resident. Thirdly, section 1(2) in itself gives no immunity from deportation, although as will be seen later, the Act substantially preserves the existing immunities of Commonwealth citizens already in the United

Kingdom. The sub-section appears to do no more than to bring the terminology applicable to those already here into line with that applicable to immigrants subsequently admitted.

(b) *The common travel area.* The 1971 Act contains a complex set of provisions, the basic purpose of which is to allow to continue the largely unregulated travel between the United Kingdom, the Republic of Ireland, the Isle of Man and the Channel Islands. Together they form a common travel area with a substantially harmonised immigration law and pratice, thus decreasing the need for internal immigration control. A person on a local journey from a place within the common travel area may enter without leave any other part, subject to refusal because of any existing deportation order in order against him, or directions received by the Secretary of State that his exclusion from the United Kingdom is in the interests of national security.[24] However, in an attempt to restrict the movement of those suspected of involvement with terrorist activities, the Prevention of Terrorism (Temporary Provisions) Act 1974 empowered the Home Secretary to provide for control over those entering or leaving Great Britain or Northern Ireland.[25] Evidence of identity and the completion of landing and embarkation cards may be demanded; wide enforcement powers of examination, detention and search now exist.[26]

The duration and conditions of a person's leave to enter and remain in one part of the common travel area will apply to his entry into the United Kingdom.[27] Similarly, a refusal of leave to enter is applicable as if made at a point of entry to the United Kingdom, and an illegal immigrant anywhere in the common travel area will be treated as such in the United Kingdom. The Secretary of State has made an Order limiting the duration and imposing conditions upon the leave of, *inter alia*, persons, other than citizens of the Republic of Ireland and patrials, who, though on a local journal from the Republic to the United Kingdom, entered the Republic, without being given leave to land, in the course of a journey to the United Kingdom from a place outside the common travel area.

The free movement of citizens of Eire to Great Britain now rests on EEC law; but the previous lack of regulation, at a time when increasingly restrictive immigration control was exercised over Commonwealth citizens, added to the suspicion that the legislation was racialist in nature. Apart from the consideration that enforcement of control over movements by Irish citizens was administratively difficult, it is also true that the policy was justified by the close ties between Ireland and the United Kingdom and the presence in the United Kingdom of large numbers of persons of Irish descent. Although not patrial, the Irish are regarded as "belongers."

Notes

1 Under s.3 the Home Secretary may prevent the entry to or exclude from Great Britain a citizen of the U.K. and Colonies unless he has been resident for the twenty years before the order or born in Great Britain, and has been ordinarily resident there throughout his life. There are no such residence limits on the power in respect of persons other than citizens of the U.K. and Colonies. Another Bill, making no major changes in these respects, was introduced in 1975.

The virtually unreviewable ground upon which this draconian power is exercisable is that the Home Secretary deems it expedient "to prevent acts of terrorism (whether in Great Britain or elsewhere) designed to influence public opinion or Government policy with respect to affairs in Northern Ireland."

2 Immigration Act s.3(9). In *R* v. *Secretary of State for Home Affairs ex p. Phansopkar* [1975] 3 W.L.R. 322, 340 Scarman L.J. was willing to assume, without deciding the point, that s.3(9) is mandatory. The Court, however, ordered the Home Secretary to entertain an application, made in the United Kingdom, for a certificate of patriality by a Commonwealth citizen under s.2(2). The Divisional Court in *Akhtar* [1975] 1 W.L.R. 1717 later held that an alien wife of a patrial, who needed leave to enter, could be excluded without an entry certificate.

3 Commonwealth Immigrants Act 1962, s.2(2)(*b*). The right did not extend

to a person against whom a deportation order was in force: s.2(5). A person was not ordinarily resident for the purpose of these provisions if there were time limitations upon his leave to remain: s.2(2)(*b*). However, workers were admitted indefinitely. s.1(2)(*a*) conferred a right of re-entry upon Commonwealth citizens ordinarily resident in the U.K. within the last two years.

In 1969 the right of entry of wives and children was made conditional upon the possession of an entry certificate; previously 1 in 40 claiming to enter were being rejected (the rate for Indians was 1 in 25). In the first four months of the new Act's operation only one holder of an entry certificate was refused and over 8,000 admitted: H.C. Deb. Vol. 791, November 11, 1969, c.227.

4   s.3(8).

5   [1974] Q.B. 313.

6   *Ibid.* at p. 801.

7   [1973] 2 All E.R. 765.

8   [1971] 1 W.L.R. 859.

9   *Shabhaz Khan* [1972] Imm. A.R. 172. A person who loses his job in the UK whilst he is abroad may thereby cease to be ordinarily resident: *Jushi* [1975] Imm.A.R.1.

10   *Afza Mussarat* [1972] Imm.A.R. 45. It has been the Government's view that more than one wife of a polygamous marriage valid by the law of the domicile could be admitted: H.C. Deb. Vol. 765, May 23, 1968, c.118-119.

11   *Muneza Bee, The Guardian*, May 21, 1974.

12   See H.C.81, para.34; H.C.79, para.39 of the rules relating to the Commonwealth citizens is to the same effect, but excepts from this requirement a wife of a Commonwealth citizen settled in the U.K. when the 1971 Act came into effect. Whilst the absence of a qualification on the wife's citizenship may appear to support the *Bee* holding, the substance of the rules clearly indicates that they relate to Commonwealth citizens.

13   According to Government estimates, from December 1967-February 1968, 1032 such children aged between 14-15 years entered to join single parent households: from the date of the introduction of the 1968 Act in March, until August 1968, only 53 such children were allowed entry. (H.C. Deb. Vol. 770, October 18, 1968, c.396).

14   H.C.79, para.13. Work permits are not required. Also those entering for a temporary purpose will be given leave to remain indefinitely: work permits are not required: H.C.80, para.25.

15   Thus a Commonwealth citizen whose grandparents left the U.K. in the early 19th century falls within the exemption: whereas a Commonwealth citizen with a U.K. born mother, but foreign-born grandparents will not if his mother had lost her U.K. citizenship before the date of his birth.

16   See for example, Annual Report of the Community Relations Commission 1972-73, para. 8(H.C. 384). On the other hand, they also benefit a large number of Anglo-Indians living in Pakistan, India and Ceylon.

17 For example, the late Mr. Norman Kirk, the Prime Minister of New Zealand, wanted equal treatment for all New Zealand citizens: *The Times*, January 31, 1973. The Melbourne newspaper, *The Age*, denied that Australians were anxious to obtain immigration privileges: *The Times*, January 4, 1973.

18 H.C.79, para.28. Extensions are only likely to be granted to those who originally entered in this capacity: *Ismail* [1973] Imm.A.R. 62. The Government felt able to extend the limit from three years to five years when, under the 1971 Act, Commonwealth citizens lost their automatic right to U.K. citizenship after five years' residence.

19 *Grant* [1974] Imm.A.R. 64.

20 For the requirements of registration applicable to aliens, see H.C.81, paras.56-57, H.C.82, paras.29-30. This was one concession made by the Government in 1971 to the argument that a measure would harm race relations. s.3(1)(c) of the Act does not restrict to non-Commonwealth citizens the power of immigration officers to impose a condition of registration.

21 Commonwealth citizens who enter as visitors or students may be granted extensions to stay on as trainees (H.C.80, para.16); it also appears easier for Commonwealth citizens to obtain extensions of their stay on training than for non-Commonwealth citizens (see H.C.80, para.15, H.C.82, para.14). Arrangements for training schemes come under the supervision of the Department of Employment, from whose decisions no appeal lies: *Latiff* [1972] Imm.A.R. 76. In the absence of a favourable report by the Department, the Home Secretary has no discretion to extend the leave: *Brizmohun* [1972] Imm.A.R. 122; *Ainooson* [1973] Imm .A.R. 43.

22 [1973] 3 All E.R. 796.

23 The only exemptions from s.3(4) are for those who are not required to obtain leave to enter, *viz.* those travelling within the common travel area, crews of ships and aircraft, members of diplomatic missions and their families, and members of specified armed forces.

24 s.1(3). A "local journey" is defined in s.11(4) which may raise some difficult questions of fact. For further details see Macdonald, *supra*, at pp.41-43.

25 s.8.

26 See S.I. 1974 Nos. 1975, 2038.

27 s.9.

Chapter 4

THE REGULATION OF IMMIGRATION

The 1971 Act reveals little of Britain's immigration policies, apart from defining those free to enter without leave and providing that others may only enter with leave of an immigration officer. The principal features of government policy are contained in the immigration rules which define the main categories of those who will normally be admitted and the conditions that may be imposed upon their leave. Home Office practice and the rulings of the immigration tribunals provide important information on interpretation and the exercise of discretion under the rules. Another important aspect of immigration policy is found in the Department of Employment's control of the work permit scheme which is not reviewable by the immigration tribunals[1] and subject to little Parliamentary scrutiny.[2]

This chapter discusses some aspects of immigration policy and administration that are not contained in the Act. The special provisions for EEC nationals coming to work in the United Kingdom are discussed in Chapter 5.

Employment

From 1962-72, the admission of workers from Commonwealth and foreign countries was regulated by distinct statutory régimes. Work permits for aliens were normally issued for no more than one year and were limited to a particular job with a named employer.[3] With the exception of the hotel and catering industries, quotas were not maintained, but permits were only issued when there was no available resident labour. The admission of alien workers was thus closely geared to the immediate needs of the labour market.

Under the 1962 Act Commonwealth citizens, in possession of an employment voucher, had a right of entry.[4] The voucher holder was admitted free of any conditions on his stay. There was thus no legal power to require the worker to continue in, or even start, the employment in respect of which the voucher was issued.[5] Originally, the voucher scheme was only intended directly to restrict the number of unskilled Commonwealth workers without jobs already arranged in the United Kingdom (*C* vouchers).[6] Severe restrictions were subsequently introduced on the global number of vouchers available either for workers with jobs to come to in the United Kingdom (*A* vouchers)[7] or with skills or qualifications of use in the United Kingdom (*B* vouchers). For example, it was announced in 1968 that applications for *B* and *A* vouchers would only be accepted for work that, in the opinion of the Ministry of Labour, was "of substantial economic or social value to the United Kingdom," unless in a manufacturing industry or if the recruitment was made through a Ministry of Labour scheme.[8]

The employment voucher system was criticised on the ground that the numerical and skill restrictions on the admission of Commonwealth workers were not justified by changes in labour demand, but were concessions to racial prejudice.[9] It was pointed out that unskilled alien workers were being admitted and that workers from the Republic of Ireland retained unrestricted access to the British labour market.[10] Indeed, the wider purposes served by employment vouchers were suggested by a Home Office Minister in 1968[11]

"The control of immigration for work by aliens is a control in the context of the labour market while the voucher for Commonwealth immigrants is not designed for that purpose. It is designed to control the rate of immigration. This is done for different purposes."

The decline in the numbers of Commonwealth workers admitted during this period reflects the diminishing quotas imposed by the Government; changes in the demand for labour, of a much less drastic kind, will be reflected in the figures in the other columns. It was also Government policy during this period to reduce the numbers of non-skilled workers coming from Commonwealth countries.[13] This, in part, explains why workers from the "old" Commonwealth represented only 5.2 per cent. in 1963 of all employment voucher holders admitted, whereas they accounted for 25 per cent. in 1972.

Whilst the statistics for alien workers must be considered in the context of the work permit system, nonetheless, in the years 1970-72 (inclusive) 24,359 alien workers were accepted for settlement after completing four years of satisfactory employment. In the same period, only 9,378 Commonwealth citizens entered with employment vouchers. Although the proportion of aliens to Commonwealth citizens accepted for settlement increased over the period, the backlog of dependants of Commonwealth citizens already resident in the United Kingdom, and the expulsion of United Kingdom passport holders from East Africa, have augmented Commonwealth settlement.[14]

The table on page 57 shows that Britain's labour force remains overwhelmingly local born and that foreign born workers are insignificantly outnumbered by those born in the Commonwealth.

The 1973 immigration rules have significantly changed the relative positions of alien and Commonwealth citizens seeking admission for employment. First, the abolition of

Table 1[12]

Admission of Workers into the United Kingdom

Year	1963	1964	1965	1966	1967	1968	1969	1970	1971	1972	1973	1974
Commonwealth citizens	30,125	14,705	12,880	5,461	4,978	4,691	4,021	4,098	3,477	1,803	2,223	2,767
Aliens	44,290	42,584	48,874	48,637	45,867	45,142	47,852	47,654	41,286	36,715	19,583	16,668
Citizens of the Republic of Ireland	32,978	39,100	40,004	44,319	33,896	30,929	27,699	27,872	20,200			

Notes to Table 1

1. From 1968 the figures for Commonwealth citizens include United Kingdom passport holders who were subject to immigration control.

2. The figures for Ireland represent those registering for the first time for National Insurance purposes: about another 40 per cent representing migrant workers, re-register each year. Figures for 1972-74 were not available to the author.

3. About 40 per cent of the work permits issued were for jobs lasting less than 12 months. The figures include trainees and student employees.

4. The figures for 1973 and 1974 do not include 6,928 and 5,785 residence permits issued to workers from EEC countries other than the Republic of Ireland.

Table 2
*Country of Origin for the Workforce
in the United Kingdom in 1971*[15]

Country of birth	United Kingdom	Republic of Ireland	Common-wealth	Others
Employees (in 1,000's)	21,856.3	442.4	574.6	586.6
Percentage of total employees in U.K.	92.8	1.8	2.9[a]	2.5[b]

Notes to Table 2

(a) 0.3 per cent. of the workers from Commonwealth countries were born in the 'old' Commonwealth.

(b) Only 0.2 per cent. had alien citizenship in 1971.

employment vouchers has deprived most Commonwealth citizens of the security of initial admission for settlement. On the other hand, some — mainly from the white Common-wealth — have benefited either from the extension of total exemption from immigration control (s.2(1)(*d*)), or the provision in the rules allowing Commonwealth citizens with a grandparent born in the United Kingdom to be admitted for settlement without a work permit.[16] Secondly, EEC nationals are now largely free to work in the United Kingdom.[17]

It is too early to assess the effects of membership of the European Communities and of extending the work permit system to Commonwealth citizens upon the pattern of labour migration to the United Kingdom. At a time of relatively high unemployment and economic difficulty, the criteria for the issue of work permits remain strict,[18] although unskilled workers are, subject to a quota, being admitted for domestic work and for the hotel and catering industries.[19] Now that the admission of Commonwealth and non-EEC workers is geared to current labour demand and the special numerical and skill limitations previously applied only to Commonwealth citizens abolished, it may be that more Commonwealth citizens will be admitted for unskilled work or for limited periods to increase their technical or commercial expertise. The recent figures show a slight increase over the previous year in the numbers of Commonwealth citizens admitted for employment, whilst the figures for aliens (including EEC nationals) significantly fell.[20] However, during the passage of the 1971 Act, and subsequently, Ministers have stated that the control of labour supply is not the only objective served by work permits. Other relevant considerations appear to include the protection of the immigrant worker from exploitation,[21] the housing, schools and social services available in the area and, no doubt, the likely effect upon race relations.[22]

The work permit scheme (including the list of permit-free employment) is not exhaustive of the categories admissible for economic activity. People admitted primarily in another category may be allowed to take employment, *e.g.* the wife and children under 18 of a man permitted to work will normally also be able to do so,[23] young Commonwealth citizens are allowed to work whilst on an extended holiday[24] and "au pair" girls.[25] Businessmen and the self-employed may also be admitted for 12 months,[26] although the Tribunal has not always found it easy to distinguish genuine business activity from disguised employment.[27] A strict view has been taken of the requirement that the business activity must produce enough to support the applicant and any dependants.[28]

Relatives

British immigration law recognises the social value attached to a person's desire to live with his family. Priority is given to the immigrant's "nuclear family" of spouse and children below the age of majority, and aged parents. Before 1973 the right of admission of the wife and children of a Commonwealth citizen resident or arriving in the United Kingdom was statutory. As part of the assimilation process of the 1971 Act, the right was relegated to the level of the immigration rules. Fears of unforeseen abuses remediable by speedy administrative changes thus outweighed the security of a statutorily protected minimum right of family unity. The claims of members of a person's "extended family" to be admitted as such are dealt with on the basis of a discretion, exercised sparingly by reference to compassion and family hardship.

The two most important exceptions to these general principles are the transitional preservation in the 1971 Act (s.1(5)) of the statutory right of admission of the wife and minor children of Commonwealth citizens settled in the United Kingdom on January 1, 1973,[29] and the more liberal provisions applicable to the dependants of EEC nationals entering for work.[30]

(a) *"Section 1(5) dependants"*

The 1962 Act provided that the wife or child under 16 of a Commonwealth citizen entering or already resident in the United Kingdom could not be refused entry unless the subject of a deportation order.[31] The 1968 Act restricted the rights of children who were not accompanying or joining both parents.[32] The principal reason given was that the right often was not being used, particularly by the Pakistani community, to facilitate family unification in the way intended, but to avoid the employment voucher scheme.[33] The changes also affected the migration of children from the

West Indies, often sent to join a single parent (generally the mother), as they got older.

A satisfactory resolution has yet to be found for the administrative problem of admitting genuine dependants with the minimum of delay and inconvenience whilst excluding the bogus. The individual carries the burden of proving dependant status.[34] In the most favourable circumstances it was foreseeable that difficulties would arise at the port of entry when the immigrant, with little understanding of the language and after a long journey from a rural country where births and marriages are inadequately documented, faced the demands of a bureaucracy accustomed to formal, reliable public records. Matters were made worse by the widespread suspicion among immigration officers that the 1962 Act was being evaded on a large scale through corruption and forgery, and by the fears of immigrants, particularly from the Indian sub-continent, that they were the victims of the racial prejudices of immigration officers.[35] The hardships caused by refusal at the port were, naturally, enormous.

More radical reforms were needed to produce a fairer administrative system than could be provided by the courts' insistence that immigration officers must fairly consider the evidence offered of dependant status.[36] In 1967 the Wilson Committee emphasised the advantages, particularly for dependants, of locally verifying the facts supporting admission to the United Kingdom. The Committee accordingly recommended that a passenger with an entry certificate, issued locally by the High Commission after a factual investigation, should be admitted unless the certificate had been obtained by fraud, it had been issued to another person, circumstances had changed since its issue or the passenger was personally unacceptable. The Committee also thought that the entry certificate procedure should remain voluntary, since aliens were decreasingly required to obtain visas.[37]

Although the Immigration Appeals Act 1969 enacted most

of Wilson's proposals, the Government inserted at the Committee stage in the House of Lords an amendment to the 1962 Act making the possession of an entry certificate a necessary qualification for entry as a dependant.[38] Even so, passengers with entry certificates can be refused on grounds wider than those apparently approved by Wilson, although they can appeal whilst still in the United Kingdom.[39]

The administration of the entry certificate system, particularly for dependants in the Indian sub-continent, has been widely criticised, particularly the increasing delays in issuing certificates.[40] In June 1975 the average time between application and interview was 22 months in Islamabad and 18 months in Dacca.[41] Whilst further increases in administrative staff may help, enormous problems are caused by bogus applications (in 1974 they were 15 per cent. of all applications for dependants' entry certificates), a public records' system inadequate to meet the demands of a Western bureaucracy and misunderstandings due to cultural differences. Suggestions for reducing the delays and the backlog of applicants include a government funded advisory service in the countries of emigration, interviews conducted in villages, and training of administrative staff in the local cultural background. A more radical proposal is that the burden of proof should be reduced; this would involve a policy shift towards fairness to the genuine dependants at some cost to efficiency in so far as it increased the rate of admission of the ineligible. A return to a voluntary entry certificate system, well publicised and run, might also go some way to separating the genuine from the bogus applications.

Although there are other variables the following table strongly suggests that the 1969 Act reduced the rate of entry of dependants, particularly from the Indian sub-continent. Whether intended or not, the 1969 Act did place an effective administrative tool in the Government's hands for regulating

Table 3

Dependants Admitted Under 1962 Act s.2

Year	1963	1964	1965	1966	1967	1968	1969	1970	1971	1972	1973	1974
										(a)	(a) (b)	(a) (b)
Total	26,234	37,460	41,214	42,026	52,813	48,650	33,820	27,407	28,014	45,494	31,250	17,800
											(b) (c)	(b) (c)
Indian sub-continent	10,278	16,197	20,020	23,005	33,681	31,543	20,387	14,789	11,666	12,725	10,100	7,850

Notes to Table 3

(a) This figure includes the dependants of the Uganda Asian refugees and other UK passport holders subject to immigration control.

(b) The new form in which from 1973 statistics are presented does not reveal the exact numbers admitted in this category.

(c) Figures include those entering from Pakistan after the Pakistan Act 1973.

the flow. In 1963 dependants comprised about 40 per cent. of all Commonwealth citizens admitted for settlement, whereas in 1973 the figure was 88 per cent.

(i) *"Wife."* For this purpose a "wife" includes a woman who entered a polygamous marriage valid by the law of the parties' domicile.[42] More surprisingly, the Tribunal has held that the wife of a citizen of Pakistan settled in the United Kingdom retained her right to admission even after the Pakistan Act 1973, which contained no transitional provisions for immigration purposes.[43] A woman living with a man on a basis regarded by local custom as permanent may be admitted as if she were his wife.[44]

(ii) *Children*. Although the statutory right of admission extends only to children under the age of 16, whose parents are settled in the United Kingdom on January 1, 1973,[45] the immigration rules extend the right to children under 18 joining their only suviving parent or the parent who has had sole responsibility for their upbringing or where the Secretary of State authorises admission because family or other considerations make exclusion undesirable.[46] Difficulties have arisen from proving age and relationship and the narrow construction of "sole responsibility." In *Emmanuel*[47] the Tribunal rejected a literal construction which would have prevented the rule from applying to the parent who had migrated before the child — the very situation envisaged by the rules. But it held that a parent had not had "sole responsibility" if any other person (*e.g.* the grandmother who had cared for the child after the mother's emigration), and not only the other parent, had shared resonponsibility. In determining the question of sole responsibility the Tribunal considers the financial support of the child, and the level of sustained interest that the parent has shown towards the child.

(b) *Spouse and children*

The most important limitation upon the right of a man to

be joined by his wife and children is that he must be able and willing to support and accommodate them without recourse to public funds.[48] No such limitation is imposed upon a husband's right to join his wife who is settled in the United Kingdom, although the deportation power looms in the background.[49] The rules apply to Commonwealth citizens and aliens alike, although the housing and financial support requirements do not apply to the dependants of Commonwealth citizens settled in the United Kingdom on January 1, 1973.[50]

In 1968 the practice was ended of allowing a man to enter by virtue of his marriage to a Commonwealth citizen settled in the United Kingdom. The reason given was that this "concession" was being abused to avoid immigration control through employment vouchers.[51] Except when they would suffer severe hardship wives should live where their husbands worked. This rule was strongly criticised because it was sexually discriminatory and caused particular hardship to women in the Pakistani, Indian and Bangladeshi communities in Britain whose parents might expect them to marry a man from their home village.[52] The anomaly became even more glaring on Britain's accession to the EEC whose rules required the admission of a worker's spouse, irrespective of sex. Thus a French woman admitted to work in the United Kingdom could be joined by her husband, but a British-born woman normally could not, unless her husband was a Commonwealth citizen with a grandparent born in the United Kingdom.

In 1974 the immigration rules were amended to admit for settlement the husband of a woman settled in the United Kingdom.[53] Elements of sexual discrimination still, however, exist in nationality and immigration law. For example, a woman admitted for a temporary purpose is not entitled to be accompanied by her husband. The "au pair" provisions only apply to females. A woman citizen of the

United Kingdom and Colonies cannot transmit citizenship to her legitimate children, nor does she by marriage confer upon her husband patrial status or a right to citizenship.[54]

The provisions for the admission of children under 18, discussed above, apply to all parents, whether admitted temporarily or for settlement, with the exception that unless the parent was settled in the United Kingdom on January 1, 1973, he must be able and willing to support and accommodate his children in the United Kingdom at his own expense.

Children over the age of 18 are normally expected to qualify for entry in their own right, but there is a discretion to admit unmarried, fully dependent sons and unmarried daughters under the age of 21 if they were a part of the family unit overseas and the whole family is being admitted or is settled in the United Kingdom.[55]

(c) *Other relatives*

Parents and grandparents over the age of retirement are admitted if they are dependent upon children settled in the United Kingdom who are able to support and accommodate them. Other "distressed" relatives may be admitted in similar circumstances, but the rules make it clear that only in the most exceptional circumstances should discretion be exercised in favour of such a relative under the age of 65.[56]

Non-patrial United Kingdom Passport Holders

From the introduction of the 1968 Act depriving United Kingdom passport holders without an ancestral connection with the United Kingdom of an unrestricted right of entry, governments have had to face the issue of balancing the constitutional propriety of a state's admitting those with no other citizenship who were hard pressed in their country of residence against such considerations as housing and school shortages in areas of potential settlement and any adverse effects upon race relations. Although the Government justified the 1968 Act by reference to the rapidly rising number of United Kingdom passport holders — mainly of Asian origin — arriving from East Africa (see Table 4 below), it is difficult to tell how far the increase in 1967 was influenced by the fear of restrictive legislation. In 1968 it was estimated that there were more than 200,000 United Kingdom passport holders, including their dependants, in East Africa. Other surveys suggest that only about 10 per cent. wished to settle in the United Kingdom, although future events in Africa and the attitudes of other countries to their admission would affect that figure.

Table 4

United Kingdom Passport Holders Admitted From East Africa

1965	1966	1967	1968	1969	1970	1971	1972	1973	1974
6,149	6,846	13,600	8,000*	6,249	6,839	11,564	34,100	12,307	10,938

*an estimated figure

Note to Table 4

No separate figures for United Kingdom passport holders were kept before 1965: the figures include dependants. The figures for 1972 include the refugees from Uganda.

Until the mass expulsion of the Asian community from Uganda, it was government policy to issue a quota of special vouchers to United Kingdom passport holders entitling them to settle.[57] Their claim ultimately to settle in the country of citizenship was not denied, but deferred.[58] Priority was given to those suffering particular hardship by, for example, being given notice to leave their country of residence by a specified date, or being barred from trade or employment. Those accepted by the Indian Government with an assurance by the British Government that they would be admitted to the United Kingdom remained eligible for a voucher, but they risked their priority status. Although those arriving without vouchers were refused entry,[59] the Government stated at the time of the 1968 Act that a person out of work and ejected from his country of residence would have to be admitted, even though he had no voucher.[60]

This latter understanding was honoured by the Conservative Government in 1972 following the Uganda expulsions; by July 1974 some 28,000 United Kingdom passport holders and their dependants had been admitted.[61] The nature of the Government's obligation to admit the Uganda Asians was questioned. In *Thakrar* v. *Secretary of State for Home Department*[62] the Court of Appeal stated that the 1971 Act excluded any possible right of admission that British protected persons, even if expelled from their country of residence with nowhere else to go, might derive from international law. However, in 1974 the European Commission on Human Rights found the exclusion of some Asian United Kingdom passport holders from Kenya to be a violation of the articles of the European Convention forbidding racial discrimination, degrading treatment and infringments of family life.[63]

The position of United Kingdom passport holders, especially in East Africa, without patriality or any other citizenship remains a source of continuing embarrassment to the Government and one of the major difficulties which any reform of United Kingdom citizenship will have to tackle.[64] The events of recent years show that it can only be resolved in co-operation with the Governments of their countries of residence and others with an ethnic and cultural interest.

Refugees

The appellant in *Thakrar* did not, apparently, challenge the refusal to admit him on the ground that it was an infringement of the provision in the immigration rules that a person should not be refused leave to enter if the only country to which he can be removed is one to which he is unwilling to go owing to well-founded fear of being persecuted for reasons of race, religion, nationality, membership of a particular social group or political opinion.[65]

Whether the exclusion of a person claiming refugee status is justiciable either by the immigration tribunals or the courts is unclear. The rule is, however, in imperative form and the tribunals have jurisdiction to reverse a decision that is, on fact or law, not in accordance with the Act or the rules. The courts have not doubted their jurisdiction to review tribunal interpretations of the rules for error of law on the face or excess of jurisdiction. One difficulty, however, is that the passenger cannot, subject to limited exceptions, appeal against his refusal before leaving the United Kingdom. Although the courts will normally not review a refusal before the statutory remedies have been exhausted[66] it could well be argued that it should exercise its discretion in favour of a claimant for refugee status, because to require a prior appeal after leaving the United Kingdom might gravely endanger his safety and liberty. But it also has to be recognised that a court might conclude that the inclusion of the right of asylum in the immigration rules was not intended to reverse the previously well-established view that this was solely a political question.[67] Finally, the 1971 Act preserves prerogative powers, which include the exclusion of aliens.[68]

The rights of admission created by the Immigration Rules are also generally subject to the personal acceptability of the individual. A passenger, otherwise qualified for admission under the rules, validly excluded on the Secretary of State's instruction because his presence is not conducive to the public good, has no right of appeal at all.[69] In these circumstances a successful challenge in the courts is unlikely, either because the passenger has no rights protected by law or because of the width of the Home Secretary's power to refuse entry.[70] An appeal does lie from the destination contained in the

directions for removal, but can only succeed where the
appellant can show that another country is willing to admit
him.[71]

The libertarian and humanitarian attitude of British
Governments in the nineteenth century towards political
refugees has continued, although there have been occasions
when concern for diplomatic relations and internal political
pressures have resulted in very questionable decisions.[72]
The importance attached to refugee status is reflected in
special administrative procedures. When a passenger claims
political asylum the immigration officer must refer the case to
Home Office headquarters. The Home Office then normally
consults the United Kingdom Representative of the United
Nations High Commissioner for Refugees and if he supports
the application, then the individual is, subject to his personal
acceptability, normally admitted.[73]

Personal Acceptability

In addition to the catch-all conducive to the public good
provision, a person otherwise qualified for admission may be
excluded on medical grounds, for a criminal conviction or
because he is the subject of a deportation order.[74] Not all
these grounds apply to all passengers. For example,
Commonwealth citizens settled in the United Kingdom on
January 1st, 1973 who qualify as returning residents can only
be refused admission if the subject of a deportation order.
The same is true of section 1(5) dependants, although the
rules extend the same protection to the wife and children of
any person settled in the United Kingdom.[75]

The width of the power to exclude because conducive to the
public good and the Home Office's reluctance to publish
more specific guidelines are open to criticism, particularly
when the exercise of the power trenches upon other values
such as freedom of thought and speech. Home Secretaries
have often stated that persons should not be refused entry

simply because of their political views; this general principle
has been said not to extend to those seeking to make
"political propaganda"[76] or to advocate violent revolution
[77] or whose presence would cause widespread offence[78] or
who are members of Communist Party "front" organisations.
Identifying "public good" with the suppression of views or
political activities of which the Government or a majority of
the people disapprove is all too easy.[79]

Notes

1   *Latiff* [1972] Imm.A.R. 76.

2   Statements of immigration rules and any amendments have to be laid
before Parliament and are subject to anulment (s.3(2)). The first set of rules
laid under the 1971 Act was indeed annulled: H.C. 846, November 22, 1972,
c.1250 *et seq.*

3   The permit could be renewed for a further three years if the worker was
still employed. After four years of satisfactory residence and employment the
worker was accepted for settlement.

4   s.2(3)(*a*). The right was subject to the worker's personal acceptability:
s.2(4)(5).

5   In 1963 efforts were made to attempt to ensure that *A* vouchers were
issued only in respect of genuine job offers and that the immigrant was
coming to do that job: H.C.686, December 19, 1963, c.264 (written answers).

6   Within a year of the passing of the Act a quota of 25 per cent. was
imposed for each country. No *C* vouchers were issued after September 1964,
when there was a waiting list of 300,000 applicants. *C* vouchers were
abolished in August 1965: *Immigration from the Commonwealth*, Cmnd.
2739 (1965).

7   Thus the 1965 White Paper (*supra*, n.6) anticipated that only 2,000 *A*
vouchers would be available.

8   H.C.759, February 26, 1968, c.242-243 (written answers). From 1971 *A*
vouchers for non-skilled work were not issued, except to Maltese: H.C.818,
May 26, 1971, c.380-381.

9   At the time in 1965 when the White Paper reduced the number of
vouchers available *per annum* from 20,800 to 8,500, the National Plan
projected a labour shortage of 0..2 million. Public services, particularly in
London, have remained well below establishment.

10 Except to Northern Ireland: Safeguarding of Employment (Northern
Ireland) Act 1947.

11 H.C.733, November 13, 1968, c.525 (Mr. Merlyn Rees).

12 The statistics for Commonwealth citizens and aliens are contained in annually published Command papers: the statistics for Irish immigrants are contained in H.C.777, February 3, 1969, c.44 (written answers) and H.C.832, March 2, 1972, c.170 (written answers).

13 During this period the shortage of N.H.S. doctors was made good largely by Commonwealth immigration; it was estimated that the number of doctors from India and Pakistan admitted to work in the U.K. was the equivalent of the output of six medical schools. For example, in 1974, 49 per cent. of all junior hospital doctors were born overseas in a Commonwealth country; in 1974, 25 per cent. of all N.H.S. doctors were born overseas.

14 In 1963, aliens were 20 per cent. of the total settlers, whilst in 1970 they were 34 per cent. H.L. 314, February 3, 1971, c.1351. An average of about 20,000 aliens were admitted and accepted for settlement each year: H.C.811, February 11, 1971, c.227.

15 Data contained in the 1971 census.

16 H.C.79, para.27. In 1973, 1,066 Commonwealth immigrants qualified under this head, and in 1974, 699.

17 H.C.81, paras.49-52.

18 See H.C.848, January 25, 1973, c.221 (written answers). The immigration rules of 1973 included doctors and dentists in the categories of workers admitted for 12 months without a work permit: H.C.79, para.29, H.C.81, para.25.

19 The quota was recently raised to 8,500 with special quotas for Maltese and U.K. passport holders: H.C.886, February 10, 1975, c.26-28 (written answers).

20 See p.92, n.8.

21 Thus both the home labour market and the immigrant worker are protected by the limitation upon the issue of work permits to jobs where the conditions of employment are not inferior to those for comparable jobs done by resident labour. In 1973 a temporary ban was imposed upon the issue of work permits for non-skilled Filipinos, following the exposure of substantial exploitation: H.C.859, July 10, 1973, 309 (written answers); *Immigrants and employment in the Clothing Industry — the Rochdale Case* (1974, Runnymede Trust).

22 The quota for hotel work has recently been described as "a total system of immigration control": H.C.867, January 15, 1974, c.358. For some years it has been government policy to encourage this industry to recruit and train resident labour.

23 H.C.79, paras.22 (students), 37 (employees, businessmen and self-employed); similar provisions apply to non-Commonwealth citizens, H.C.81, paras. 20, 33.

24 H.C.79, para.28. Since the "holiday" may last for five years, this is a significant advantage of Commonwealth citizenship for those able to take

advantage of it. For the employment to be "incidental" to the primary purpose of the holiday, "a person must have some resources with which to finance his holiday, augmenting such resources from time to time by taking employment." *Grant* [1974] Imm.A.R. 64, 68.

25 H.C.79, para.23, H.C.81, para.21. Commonwealth citizens became admissible as "au pairs" for the first time under the current immigration rules. About 6,000 "au pairs" are admitted each year.

26 H.C.79, paras.31-36; H.C. 81, paras.27-32.

27 In *Pritpal Singh* [1972] Imm.A.R. 154 the appellant, a company director with a minority shareholding in a company for which he received only a salary was held not to qualify. In *Ally* [1972] Imm.A.R.258, the Tribunal stressed the importance of the investment of the applicant's own money in the business.

28 In *Martin* [1972] Imm.A.R. 275 the Divisional Court upheld the Tribunal's ruling that other sources of unearned income could not be taken into account, even though together the applicant could support herself without taking employment. But see *Stawczykowska* [1972] Imm.A.R. 220.

29 This will presumably not include the beneficiaries of Mr. Jenkins' amnesty; they will be "settled" from the date on which their position was regularised by the grant of indefinite leave to remain.

30 See Chap.5.

31 s.2(2), (5).

32 1962 Act, s.2A.

33 In 1967, 12,666 children under 16 entered from Pakistan (about 30 per cent. of all children admitted from the new Commonwealth). But since about 67 per cent. of *all* dependants from the new Commonwealth are from Pakistan this figure is not surprising. Moreover, only 37 per cent. of all Pakistani dependants were children; whereas for the new Commonwealth as a whole children comprised over 70 per cent. of all dependants admitted in that year. The Government may have been on stronger ground when pointing out that in December 1967, about 30 per cent. of all dependent children from Pakistan were boys aged between 14-15, joining male households. The Government's inability to tackle this "abuse" until 6 months after it was first detected was used in 1971 as justification for removing the statutory basis of the admision of dependants.

34 1971 Act s.3(8), confirming this interpretation of 1961 Act, s.2(2) in *Re K.(H.)* [1967] 2 Q.B. 617.

35 Disciplinary action was taken against eight immigration officers who wrote a letter to the press supporting Mr. Enoch Powell's views on immigration policy: H.C.765, May 21, 1968, c.69-70 (written answers). In 1972 a Minister agreed that an advertisement for immigration officers that stated, "Britain, like the best hotels, clubs and restaurants cannot afford to allow everyone through its doors," should be withdrawn. Government recruitment policy was also criticised on the ground that advertisements for

immigration officers appeared only in the more right-wing newspapers: H.C.839, June 22, 1972, c.174 (written answers).

36 *Re K.* (*H.*)[1967] 2 Q.B. 617; *Re A.* [1968] 2 All E.R. 145. But in *Alibhai* [1972] Imm. A.R. 127 the Tribunal held that the entry certificate officer was not acting quasi-judicially and was free to discuss the case with his superior. The administrative requirement that applicants for employment vouchers specify their dependants was not effective.

37 Report of the Committee on Immigration Appeals, Cmnd.3387 (1967), paras.74-76.

38 1969 Act, s.20. The Government was alarmed at the rate of refusals, — in 1968, the year after Wilson reported, double that in 1967 — particularly of citizens from India and Pakistan. Entry certificate holders were very seldom rejected. Dependants of aliens also require entry clearance in the form of a visa or a Home Office letter of consent: H.C. 81, paras.9, 10.

39 1971 Act, s.13(3).

40 See *Control of Commonwealth Immigration* (1970), summarising the evidence taken by the Select Committee on Race Relations and Immigration 1969-70. For a vivid and thoughtful eye-witness account, see Akram and Leigh, *Where Do You Keep Your String Beds?* (1974, Runnymede Trust). Certificates are issued in the order applications are received, with priority given to newly-married couples and cases of extreme hardship. No such delays occur with entry certificates issued for other purposes, e.g. visits, business or study. The delays involved in the issue of certificates of patriality in the Indian sub-continent were sharply criticised judicially in *Phansopkar supra.*

41 H.C. 895, July 18, 1975, c.627-628 (written answers). If further inquiries are made in the U.K., or an appeal is lodged, delays are much longer.

42 *Afza Mussarat* [1972] Imm.A.R. 45; a child whose adoption is not recognised by the law of the parties' domicile has no right of entry: *Malik* [1972] Imm. A.R.37, *Merchant* [1975] Imm.R.49. This is a necessary but not sufficient condition, H.C.79, para.43, *Singh* [1975] Imm.A.R.34.

43 *Munez Bee, The Guardian*, May 21, 1974. The rights conferred by the 1962 Act appear to apply only when the dependants and the sponsor are Commonwealth citizens.

44 H.C.79, para.42; H.C.81, 37. See *Hessing* [1972] Imm.A.R.134.

45 in *Pinnock* [1974] Imm.A.R.22 the Tribunal stated that the purpose of the right was to enable families to be united and that the child, therefore, had to be joining both parents. Despite the clear wording of the 1962 Act s.2, it was not enough that both parents resided in the U.K.

46 H.C.79, paras.39,43. "Parent" can include an adoptive parent and an illegitimate child's mother and putative father. But note that citizenship does not descend from a putative father.

47 [1972] Imm.A.R.69.

48 H.C.79, para. 39, H.C.81, para. 34. The only exception is that seasonal

workers have no right to be joined by their family; permits are not normally issued for residential domestic work to those with dependants: H.C.79, para. 37, H.C.81, para.33.

49 H.C.79, para.47 (as amended by Cmnd. 5715), H.C.81, para.42 (as amended by Cmnd. 5717).

50 This was the importance of *Munez Bee* (*supra*, n.43); the appellant's husband was in prison.

51 In 1968, 1,676 Commonwealth citizens in this category were admitted.

52 Although in 1974 there were 38,000 unmarried women who might theoretically enter an arranged marriage, it was estimated that in fact relatively few would. H.C.79, paras,48, 49 made it difficult for fiancés to enter the U.K. U.K. passport holders from Uganda were not allowed to be joined by their husbands: this was revised early in 1974 by Mr. Jenkins.

53 Fiancés are admitted for 3 months and the conditions removed on marriage: H.C.79, para.48 (as amended by Cmnd. 5715), H.C.81, para.43 (as amended by Cmnd. 5717). In 1974, 7,753 Commonwealth citizens were accepted for settlement as spouses, of whom about one third were men. The figure for aliens was 7,470 of whom nearly half were men.

54 However, a woman married and registered as a citizen by virtue of her marriage under *BNA* s.6(2) after the passing of the 1971 Act does not thereby become patrial: 1971 Act s.2(2). But a Commonwealth citizen may be patrial by virtue of his mother's citizenship of the U.K. and Colonies by birth in the United Kingdom or Islands: 1971 Act s.2(1)(d).

55 H.C.79, para.44, H.C.81, para.39. A family may remain a "unit" even though the members are physically separated: *Pereira* [1972] Imm.A.R.224, cf. *Patel* [1972] Imm.A.R.59.

56 H.C.79, paras.45, 46, H.C.81, paras.40, 41. The age requirement does not apply to a widowed mother or to one of two parents travelling together.

57 In 1968, the voucher annual quota was 1,500; in 1971 and 1972 the quota was increased. The issue of these vouchers was outside the appeals provision of the 1969 Act (*Shah* [1972] Imm.A.R.56), although extra-statutory appeals were heard locally.

58 H.C.759, February 27, 1968, c.1256.

59 Between March 1968 and January 1971, 42 U.K. passport holders' without vouchers were refused. The plight of those shuttle-cocked between airports or exhausting their funds in European hotels aroused deep anxiety.

60 H.C.759, February 27, 1968, c.1501; H.L.289, February 29, 1968, c.1169.

61 See Humphry and Ward, *Passports and Politics* (1974) for a full account. A statement by the Home Secretary, Mr. Carr, threw doubts on the Government's willingness to take similar action in the future: H.C. 849, January 25, 1973, c.656.

62 [1972] Q.B. 684; see (1975) 37 M.L.R. 72. The reasoning should also

apply to all U.K. passport holders not otherwise qualified to enter. The case was decided on the ground that the appellant had not established that he was a British protected person. Lord Denning M.R. also doubted whether even in international law the British Government was obliged to admit the victims of mass expulsion of its "nationals" whose status was acquired through a connection with an overseas territory.

63 The Commission decided not to take the case to the Human Rights Court: *The Times* June 29 and 31, 1974.

64 In 1974 the quota of special vouchers issued was raised to 5,000; perhaps in anticipation of changes in U.K. citizenship law, as Mr. Jenkins said "that it was likely that all U.K. passport holders in East Africa who wished to come to the U.K. would have done so by 1979: H.C.890, April 14, 1975, c.23 (written answers).

65 H.C.79, para.54, H.C.81, para.55. The Aliens Act 1905 s.1(3) protected political and religious refugees although the Secretary of State, not the Board, decided whether the appellant had committed an offence of a *political* character: s.8(4).

66 *R.v. Peterkin ex p. Soni* [1972] Imm.A.R. 253.

67 See, e.g. *ex p. Soblen* [1963] 2 Q.B. 243, 303, and the remarks of Lord Denning M.R. in *Ali* [1973] Imm.A.R.33, 34. But an *ex parte* injunction has been granted to prevent the removal of Chilean refugees: see, *Goldstein, The Times*, January 2, 1974.

68 s.33(5). Moreover, since the rules are not delegated legislation they may only create rights enforceable in the courts through being binding upon the tribunals.

69 1971 Act s.13(5). The Home Secretary's certificate is conclusive, s.18(2).

70 See *Soblen* (*supra*) and *Schmidt* [1969] 1 All E.R. 904. *Quarere*, whether a person who is prima facie qualified under the rules, but who is excluded on the non-conducive ground and has not concealed information in applying for entry clearance, does not have a legitimate expectation that he will be admitted. See *Van Duyn* v. *Home Office* [1974] 1 W.L.R. 1107.

71 *Ali* [1973] Imm.A.R.33.

72 For example, General Delgado, a subsequently murdered political opponent of the Portuguese Government was refused political asylum because he entered from Brazil: H.C.684, November 20, 1963, c.990-992. In 1974 Mr. Jenkins admitted political refugees from Chile even though they had entered from another country: H.C.878, July 29, 1974, c.85 (written answers). Recently, the Home Secretary has made the conditions for the admission of political refugees from Vietnam and Chile more stringent: H.C.891, May 8, 1975, c.498 (written answers), H.C.892, May 16, 1975, c.199 (written answers). The former require a prior link with the U.K. and the latter a reliable sponsor. See also the Moroccan officers' affair of 1972 (see Chap. 6, n.40).

73 H.L.355, December 3, 1974, c.58-59. The Immigration Appeals

(Procedure) Rules 1972 S.I.No.1684 para.7(3) provides that the U.K. Representative may become a party to an appeal when refugee status is claimed.

74 H.C.79, paras.58-63, H.C.81, paras.60-65. The criminal offence must be within the First Schedule of Extradition Act 1870. This might require the tribunal to consider whether the offence was of a political character.

75 1962 Act, s.2(2)(5), although they may be required to report to a medical officer; H.C.79, para.60 (as amended by Cmnd. 5715), H.C.81, para.62 (as amended by Cmnd. 5717). The grounds for refusing a man leave to enter or remain as the husband of a woman settled in the U.K. are wider; *Vasiljevic* [1975] Imm.A.R.100.

76 Mr Callaghan refused visas to representatives of the South Vietnam Liberation Students Union on this ground; he distinguished them from those making "a positive contribution to peace in Vietnam." HC 775, December 19, 1968, c.442-443 (written answers). The N.L.F. representative at the Paris conference, Mme. Binh, was, however, admitted to attend a C.N.D. rally: H.C.777, February 13, 1969, c.1552.

77 Those who have given support to the illegal Rhodesian régime are also excluded, although Mr. Ian Smith's son was admitted as an industrial trainee: H.C.806, November 12, 1970, c.241-242 (written answers). See Southern Rhodesian (Immigration Act 1971) Order 1972, S.I. No. 1583.

78 In recent years visits by South African sports teams have been opposed on this ground. In 1975 the Home Secretary said that this was no reason to refuse a visa to Mr. Shelepin, despite the "offence" caused by his presence to certain sections of the public. The possibility of serious public disorder is also a particular consideration.

79 See Sir John Foster's Report of the *Enquiry Into The Practice And Effects of Scientology* (1971), criticising the exclusion of scientologists. 181 scientologists have been refused leave to enter to work, study or engage in the business of scientology: H.L. Deb.vol.366, December 2, 1975, c.474.

Chapter 5

IMMIGRATION AND THE EEC

It is a striking irony that the Immigration Act 1971 came into effect and Britain's membership of the European Communities commenced on the same day, January 1, 1973. For whilst the 1971 Act completed the processes started in 1962 of widening the scope of immigration control over British subjects and restricting the conditions upon which they were admissible, the European Communities Act 1972 extended to Britain the EEC's liberal provisions for ensuring the free movement of people within the Community. Modification of two of the cardinal principles underlying the 1971 Act was necessary in order to comply with EEC law. First, that all non-patrials should for immigration purposes be treated alike, irrespective of nationality.[1] Secondly, that the admission of workers and the conditions attached to their leave to remain should be closely related to current labour demands. The swing towards Europe and away from the Commonwealth in political, social and economic matters is nowhere more vividly manifested than in Britain's immigration laws.

This chapter will examine the principal features of EEC immigration law and its impact upon the United Kingdom.

Background

Article 3 of the Treaty of Rome envisages the abolition of restrictions upon free movement of persons and services as one means of achieving the EEC's overall aims of increasing economic expansion, raising of living standards and encouraging closer relations between Member States. The prohibition of discrimination on the ground of nationality in respect of activities within the Treaty's scope is a basic principle of the Treaty.[2] Within this general framework the Treaty makes more specific provisions for the attainment of its objectives.

The Treaty is primarily concerned to secure the free movement of people within the Community for such economic purposes as employment, setting up business, exercising a profession or rendering services in a self-employed capacity. To this end EEC law generally requires Member States to abolish legal restrictions upon the entry or residence of those so engaged and upon their freedom of access to employment. The prohibition of discrimination against EEC nationals and their families in Member States in such matters as employment, housing and education applies equally to public authorities and private individuals.[3] EEC law also contains positive measures to encourage free movement. For example, legislative powers are conferred upon the Council of Ministers to ensure that workers are not disadvantaged in matters of social security by working in another Member State,[4] to establish machinery for matching job vacancies to job seekers,[5] and to provide for the mutual recognition in Member States of diplomas, certificates and other evidence of qualifications.[6]

There is no doubt that the EEC has been very successful in creating a liberal structure of law enabling individuals to cross national frontiers to maximise their own standard of living. Although tempered by other social policies,[7] the underlying free market philosophy that the most efficient allocation of resources is achieved by allowing capital and labour to move to where the returns are highest, has been criticised. In particular, it can be argued that much more emphasis should be placed on taking employment to the people, especially through increased Community aids to the poorer regions.

It is difficult to assess the impact that the liberalised EEC law has had upon the patterns of migration within the Community,[8] for whilst the volume has increased, so has the volume of workers entering from outside the Community. For example, in 1958 there were 50,000 EEC nationals employed in the Federal Republic of Germany and almost twice as many foreign workers from other countries; in 1972 there were over half a million EEC nationals and over one and a half million workers from outside the EEC. In France the number of EEC nationals employed has actually decreased since the liberalisation, whilst the number of non-EEC nationals has increased. It has been suggested that the legal liberalisation has only had a significant impact upon countries that previously adopted a very restrictive policy and that the level of supply and demand for labour remains the most important factor affecting the volume of movement. The housing shortage prevalent in most European industrial conurbations is another important limitation upon migration and this has broadly the same effect irrespective of the worker's nationality.

The conditions under which many migrant workers live and work, and the social problem thereby caused, has recently attracted the attention of the Commission. It has been suggested that Member States should co-ordinate their immigration policies and that the benefits of EEC law should be extended to all workers in the Community, irrespective of nationality, starting with those from the asociated states.[9] The Commission has also raised the issue of extending political rights to EEC nationals in other Member states; this could form the basis of a new Community citizenship.

The Scope of EEC Law
The Treaty is surprisingly vague about the scope of the

application of the free movement provisions, even though the Court has held them to be directly applicable.[10] Article 48 speaks of free movement of workers "within the Community,"[11] and the Community is defined as the Member States and those European territories for whose external affairs the Member States are responsible[12]; the free movement provisions have been extended to the French Overseas Departments.[13] Otherwise the free movement of workers from overseas countries and territories in the Member States is governed by agreements yet to be made.[14] On the accession of the United Kingdom the territorial scope of the Treaty was limited to Great Britain, Northern Ireland and Gibraltar; the Channel Isles and the Isle of Man were subject to special provisions but were not included for the purpose of the free movement of persons.[15]

Uncertainties also exist in identifying the beneficiaries of the free movement provisions within the territorial scope of the Treaties. Article 48(1) speaks only of "workers," although the prohibition in the second paragraph of discrimination based on nationality between workers of Member States may indicate that the scope of the Article was intended to be confined to nationals of Member States.[16] Indeed, by impliedly excluding workers from overseas countries and territories, the free movement provisions may not even extend to nationals of Member States who derive their nationality from connection with an overseas territory. [17] The implementing legislation refers to "nationals" of Member States, irrespective of their residence.[18]

If the scope of the Treaty is limited to nationals, the European Court will probably leave the law of each Member State to identify its own nationals. But difficulties may be encountered in determining whether a person who is a national under the law of a Member State is also "from" an overseas territory and, therefore, whilst exempt from national immigration control, not entitled to free movement within the

Community. On the one hand, the Court may adopt a very restrictive view, holding that a person who acquired his nationality by his connection with an overseas territory can only benefit from free movement by virtue of an agreement made under Article 135. Alternatively, it may hold that employment free of restrictions within a Member State brings him within Article 48.

The complexities of applying these provisions to the United Kingdom were manifest; for British law does not recognise the status of "United Kingdom national," and exemption from immigration control neither extends to all with citizenship of the United Kingdom and Colonies nor is it confined to those with that citizenship. Furthermore, entitlement to civic and political rights extends to all residents with the status of British subject, irrespective of citizenship and immigration status, and to citizens of Eire. The British Government, in a unilateral Declaration annexed to the Treaty of Accession, defined United Kingdom nationals, for the purpose of Community law, as those citizens of the United Kingdom and Colonies and British subjects without the citizenship of a Commonwealth country who are patrial, and persons who acquired United Kingdom and Colonies citizenship by birth, registration or naturalisation in Gibraltar or whose father did. The most significant groups excluded from this definition are those Commonwealth citizens patrial by virtue of the 1971 Act, s.2(1)(*d*) and s.2(2), Commonwealth citizens settled in the United Kingdom, and citizens of the United Kingdom and Colonies (mostly from East Africa) who have been resident for less than five years. Because the Channel Islands and the Isle of Man did not wish all the provisions of the Treaty of Rome to apply to them, patrials whose status depends solely upon their or their parents' or grandparents' birth in the Islands are excluded from EEC law on the free movement of persons.[19] The Treaty of Accession also qualifies the territorial scope of

Community law by providing that the free movement
provisions shall not apply to Ireland or Northern Ireland for
at least five years.[20]

It has been argued that the United Kingdom Declaration is
inconsistent with the provisions of the Treaty of Rome and
that, in addition, it is objectionable because racially
discriminatory. If Articles 48 and 49 are limited to nationals
of Member States, rather than, say, those residing in Member
States free of conditions, it would seem unlikely that the
European Court would, in the absence of a definition of a
United Kingdom national in British law, declare invalid the
definition propounded by the British Government in the
Treaty of Accession.[21]

Nonetheless, it can be argued that the provisions of EEC
law, whether contained in the Treaty or legislation made
under it, are to be read subject to those notions of human
rights that are part of the common tradition of the Member
States.[22] Moreover, the Court has recently stated that
international treaties for the protection of human rights on
which the Member States have collaborated or of which they
are signatories can be used as guides to the content of those
rights.[23] It will be recalled that the Commission on Human
Rights, in a case brought by a United Kingdom passport
holder from East Africa refused entry to the United
Kingdom, found the United Kingdom Government to be in
breach, *inter alia*, of the prohibition against racial discrimination.[24] It might, therefore, be maintained that whilst the
term "national" is normally to be interpreted by reference to
the law of the Member State, this does not, as a matter of
Community law, enable the State to exclude residents holding
its passport who have no other citizenship and no legal right
to reside elsewhere.

The evidence does not put the Community above suspicion
of racial discrimination.[25] For whilst the Commission
originally appeared satisfied with a wide definition of United

Kingdom nationals, some hostility, especially from German and Dutch politicians, to extending free movement to Britain's black population was reported. Whilst it is true that many United Kingdom passport holders and Commonwealth citizens of non-European origin are excluded by the Unilateral Declaration, so also are section 2(1)(*d*) patrials. But it should also be remembered that after five years' residence in the United Kingdom most of those Commonwealth citizens will be eligible for free movement,[26] as, of course, will their children who are born here. It is perhaps this eventuality that accounts for that opaque Joint Declaration in the Treaty of Accession, which provides that if social difficulties arise after the enlargement of the Community from the free movement of workers, the Member States reserve the right to bring the matter for resolution to the institutions of the Community.

Right of Entry

An EEC national has a right to enter another Member State for work whether as an employee or as a self-employed person,[27] unless he is personally unacceptable to the national authorities.[28] The right to enter is exercisable simply on the production of a passport or valid identity card. EEC law also requires the Member State, of which the person wishing to work within the Community is a national, to allow him to leave and to issue him, in accordance with its laws, with a passport or identity card.[29]

As a matter of Community law the term "worker" can include a person not currently employed, but who is able and willing to work,[30] even though the Treaty is primarily aimed at those who are seeking entry in order to accept an offer of employment.[31] The right to enter is extended, irrespective of nationality, to the principal entrant's spouse, children who are under 21 or dependent, and the dependent parents and grandparents of the worker and spouse.[32]

These rights of entry were implemented by special
overriding provisions in the immigration rules[33]; the 1971
Act expressly preserved the Home Secretary's freedom to
frame his instructions to immigration officers in terms that
took account of nationality or citizenship.[34] Whilst these
amendments were necessary in order to comply with Treaty
obligations,[35] since the EEC provisions are probably
directly applicable,[36] an EEC national refused entry in
contravention of Community law, could in any event
challenge the legality of his exclusion in a British court, by
virtue of the European Communities Act 1972.[37] The
immigration rules confer a right of entry upon workers
entering both to seek and to take employment and leave to
remain for six months is to be given to those not already in
possession of a residence permit. The treatment given to
dependants under EEC law is strikingly more generous than
that given to dependants of Commonwealth citizens under the
immigration rules.

Right of Residence

EEC law confers a general right upon EEC nationals to reside
in the Member State where they are workers or self-employed
persons.[38] The right extends to their families irrespective of
nationality; this is subject to an apparently contradictory
requirement that the worker must have accommodation for
his family, although this must not give rise to discrimination
between national and EEC workers.[39]

Member States are required to issue residence permits valid
for at least five years, and automatically renewable, to
workers who present the document with which they obtained
entry and a statement that they are employed there.[40]
Moreover, a residence permit may not be revoked simply
because the worker becomes unemployed — unless he is able
but refuses to work — although if at the time of the first
renewal of the permit the worker has been involuntarily

unemployed for more than 12 months, the new residence permit may be restricted to 12 months.[41] Temporary permits limited to the period of expected employment are issued to those whose employment is not expected to last for more than 12 months.

The right of residence does not end when the worker ceases to be employed upon reaching the age of retirement or when unable to work because of some permanent disability.[42] If he satisfies the relatively short prior residence requirements, he has a right of permanent residence; he may claim the right at any time within two years of acquiring it, and absence abroad for less than six consecutive months does not affect the validity of the permit issued when the right is exercised. The worker's right continues in the surviving spouse who also has an independent right of permanent residence if the worker, after residing in that state for two years, dies from an industrial accident or occupational disease during his working life. It has been suggested that this legislation may be *ultra vires* in that it confers rights upon people who are neither workers, because they are no longer able to work, nor members of a worker's family. But these objections are unlikely to be sustained since the legislation has a rational connection with the broad purposes envisaged by the Treaties. For the absence of a guarantee of continued residence for the worker and his surviving family may sensibly be regarded as an obstacle to the free movement of workers.[43]

The British immigration rules on control after entry embody the principal features of this legislation[44]; they also contain the understanding by the Council of Ministers that an EEC national who enters in order to seek work may be treated as a tourist who has overstayed his leave, if, after six months, he has not obtained employment or has in that time become a charge on public funds.[45] The rules do not appear to limit the right of the worker's family to reside with him by

reference to the availability of accommodation,[46] and it is
arguable that a refusal on this ground could be set aside, even
though not required by EEC law. The anomaly that other
EEC nationals working in the United Kingdom were entitled
to be joined by their husbands, whereas British women were
not, was an impetus to the amendments to the rules made in
1974.[47]

Equality of Opportunity

A fundamental principle of EEC law for securing the free
movement of persons is that there shall be no discrimination
against EEC nationals on the ground of nationality in any
way that may hinder the freedom to pursue work or
self-employment within the Community.[48]

Since British law does not generally prohibit discrimination
on this ground,[49] and since no specific legislative changes
have been made to implement the relevant EEC provisions,
rights enforceable in British courts will have to be derived
directly from EEC law, under the European Communities
Act 1972.[50] However, the European Court has recently
made it clear that a Member State may be in default of Treaty
obligations if it fails to amend discriminatory legislation
which contains an apparent bar on the employment of EEC
nationals in contravention of directly applicable Community
law.[51] For even though the national legislation is in fact not
invoked against EEC nationals, its very existence may deter
EEC nationals from seeking the apparently prohibited
employment. Such statutes as contained discriminatory
provisions on matters within the scope of the Treaty are
rendered inoperative, at least, against EEC nationals by the
1972 Act[52]; this may suffice to comply with the Treaty,
although not specifically to repeal such provisions may cause
confusion.

Apart from the differences between EEC law and the Race
Relations Act 1968 on the prohibited grounds of

discrimination there are other significant divergencies. EEC law contains no exceptions equivalent to those in the 1968 Act, for example, relating to employment in private households, [53] the letting of small premises,[54] or in the provision for segregated sleeping accommodation by employees on board merchant ships.[55] Whereas the 1968 Act provides for conciliation and ultimately enforcement only by the Race Relations Board, before specially constituted county courts, and sets up a complex mechanism for the adjudication of allegations of discrimination in matters of employment largely outside the courts, the rights derived from EEC law are presumably enforceable, for example, by normal proceedings for declaration or injunction in the ordinary courts.

Discrimination on the ground of nationality is prohibited under EEC law in employment, conditions of work, terms of service, membership of a trade union, housing, vocational training and education for the worker's children.[56] For example, in *Marsman*, [57] the European Court held that a Dutch national working in Germany could not validly be dismissed on a ground not applicable to German nationals. In *Alaimo*,[58] the European Court held that a refusal on the ground of nationality by a French Prefect of an educational grant to the daughter of an Italian working in France was a violation of Regulation 1612/68, Article 12. Two recent cases have extended the scope of discrimination in important ways. In *Van Binsbergen*,[59] the Court held that a Dutch law requiring that legal advisers — whose activities were otherwise subject to no regulation — who appeared before administrative tribunals must be resident in the Netherlands, violated EEC law. For even though the purpose of this law may have been to protect clients, its effect was to discriminate on the grounds of nationality and it violated the right of non-residents to provide services across national frontiers. Since EEC law only requires EEC nationals to be treated no less favourably than nationals of the Member State, it is quite open for a Member State to require persons to belong to a professional association or to hold certain qualifications.[60] Moreover, the Court stated that a requirement that legal advisers should have a professional address within the jurisdiction of the tribunal would be acceptable if rationally related to the protection of the public and the better administration of justice.

In *Walrave and Koch*[61] the Court held that a rule of an international cycling association, to which bodies from EEC and elsewhere belonged, might be unenforceable under Community law insofar as it required the "pace-maker" to be of the same nationality as the cyclist. A striking feature of this decision is that the rule related to a competition to be held outside the Community; but the Court appeared to find prohibited discrimination in the fact that the inability to compete in the competition would adversely affect their employment opportunities in other events held within the Community. The Court also made it clear that the prohibitions against discrimination directly apply to public authorities and private individuals and thus confer rights enforceable in national courts by the victims of discrimination. Thus, for example, it is unlawful for a local authority and a private landlord to discriminate against an EEC national working in the United Kingdom on the ground of his nationality. The paradoxical situation might thus arise of a landlord's arguing that he refused to let to a black French natinal because of his colour and not his nationality!

Nonetheless, there are some important limitations to the right to equal treatment. Since EEC nationals do not have political rights in Member States, the Treaty does not apply to employment in the public service nor to activities by a self-employed person that involve the exercise of official authority.[62] The scope of these exceptions is difficult to assess, especially for the United Kingdom which lacks the sharp distinction drawn in European law between public and private law.[63] But it is very doubtful whether a state may exclude EEC nationals from industrial employment by a government body.[64] The Court has recently held that a state may not exclude EEC nationals from a profession because some of the activities involve the exercise of official authority. Its discrimination must be limited to those activities.[65] Discrimination against EEC nationals is allowed when the nature of a particular job requires particular linguistic knowledge.[66]

In order to supply the information necessary to encourage optimal free movement, the EEC has created a cumbersome machinery at Community level to match labour vacancies in Member States to applications for employment within the Community.[67] This scheme was also intended, subject to some exceptions, to ensure that EEC nationals got priority over workers from outside the Community.[68] The scheme has, however, proved of limited practical importance, since employers have by-passed it by direct recruitment. Although the Treaty does not provide for the suspension of free movement, either by the institutions of the Community or by unilateral action of a Member State, the Commission may, at the request of a Member State, suspend the matching procedures during a time of disturbance in the local labour market.[69] Thus, contrary to previous British practice, the EEC law leaves control of immigration of workers largely to the operation of market forces.

Personal Acceptability

Community law does enable Member States to refuse admission or continued residence to an EEC national if his presence will be a threat to public policy, security or health.[70] These terms have to an extent been limited by subsequent legislation intended to co-ordinate the permitted grounds of refusal.[71] Thus an exhaustive list of diseases and disabilities justifying initial exclusion has been compiled.[72]

The scope of public policy and security have also been limited, although much less precisely. The negative limitations are that the power may not be exercised to serve economic ends,[73] nor solely because of past criminal convictions. The positive indication of the scope of the power is that its exercise shall be based solely on the personal conduct of the individual concerned.[74]

Two recent cases before the European Court have raised important issues on the interpretation of the scope of public policy. In *Van Duyn* v. *Home Office* [75] the plaintiff, a Dutch national, was refused entry to the United Kingdom to take employment with the Church of Scientology. The decision was made in pursuance of the Government's policy of discouraging the organisation which it considered "socially harmful." On the first reference under Article 177 from a British court,[76] the European Court held Article 48 of the Treaty and Article 3(1) of Directive 64/221 were directly applicable and, therefore, conferred rights upon individuals that they could assert in national courts. The Court's reasoning is not entirely satisfying. For whilst it emphasised that derogations from the fundamental principle of free movement should be narrowly and uniformly construed, the Court also conceded the absence, outside the economic sphere, of any Community concept of public policy. It thus left Member States largely free to formulate their own notions of what conduct should be treated as contrary to public policy. It held that the "personal conduct of the individual" could include present membership of an organisation regarded by national authorities as socially harmful. It is unfortunate that the Court did not mention its earlier judgments in which it stated that Community law should be interpreted in the light of those notions of fundamental human rights that are part of the common tradition of the Member States.[77] For to refuse entry on public policy grounds because the Government disapproves of the views lawfully expressed by the organisation to which the alien belongs, clearly raises important issues of freedom of speech and association. *Van Duyn* was surely a suitable case in which the Court could have demonstrated that economic freedom was not the only individual right protected by Community law.

The Court's judgment in *Bonsignore*[78] is somewhat in contrast with its interpretation of the scope of the "personal conduct" provision in *Van Duyn*. For the Court held that it was unjustifiable to deport an EEC national after a criminal conviction, if the reason for the decision was to deter other foreigners from committing crimes in the host country. Can it not equally be said that the Home Office's exclusion of Miss Van Duyn was aimed at generally discouraging the activities of Scientologists, rather than at preventing any harm that she herself might do?[79] But the Court, in a very brief judgment, appears to have dodged the second and more important question raised in *Bonsignore*, namely whether an EEC national may be deported to punish him for offences already committed, or simply to prevent him from committing offences in the future. Advocate-General Mayras seems to conclude that the power may only be exercised on the latter ground:[80] the Court said no more than that personal but not general deterrence of others was lawful.

There is no doubt that the powers contained in British immigration law to refuse entry or to deport because the decision is deemed conducive to the public good, are wider than is permissible under EEC law. Although the immigration rules do not make special provision for the exclusion or deportation of EEC nationals, insofar as EEC law is directly applicable, an EEC national can challenge the legality of the decision before the appellate authorities or in the High Court.[81] For example, EEC nationals may not be deported on the ground of illness occurring after they have received residence permits.[82] The wife of an EEC national cannot be deported in a "family deportation" order if she herself is employed here.

Notes

1 The 1971 Act was, of course, primarily concerned to assimilate non-patrial Commonwealth citizens and aliens for immigration purposes. s.3(2) made it clear that the immigration rules could distinguish on the ground of nationality or citizenship.

2 Art. 7. Although it is unclear whether this is directly applicable, the Court has held that the anti-discriminatory provisions in the Treaty and legislation dealing with free movement of persons are. See *infra* at p.86.

3 *Walrave and Koch* v. *U.C.I.* (Court of Justice of the European Communities, Case 36/74).

4 Art. 51, Reg. 1408/71.

5 Art. 49; the details of this scheme are contained in Reg. 1612/68.

6 Art. 57; it applies only to the self-employed, although the same problems may arise for employees. For details of progress, see Lipstein, *The Law of the EEC* (1974), pp.142-145. Agreement has been reached recently on a minimum educational requirement to allow doctors free movement. Doctors educated outside the Community — *e.g.* many of the Asian doctors in the U.K. — are thereby excluded.

7 For example, the European Social Fund, reformed by Reg. 2396/71, may, for example, make grants for training workers in new skills, the reduction of unemployment of a long term structural nature and for encouraging employment in less developed regions.

8 See, further, W.R. Böhning, *The Migration of Workers in the U.K. and the European Community* (1972), especially Chap. 3. In 1973, 6,928 residence permits were issued in the U.K. to workers from the EEC (excluding Ireland), 10,978 aliens (excluding EEC nationals) and 1,471 Commonwealth citizens entered with work permits for 12 months or more. In 1974, the figures for each category were 5,785, 8,765 and 1,988.

9 The Association Agreements with Greece and Turkey both provide for the eventual extension of free movement of workers, but the Yaoundé Convention between the EEC and 18 African states includes the right of establishment, but not the free movement of workers.

10 *Van Duyn* v. *Home Office* [1974] C.M.L.R. 1 (Art. 48).

11 But it would surely be odd to require a national of a Member State residing outside the Community to enter his own country before he could take a job in another Community country with the benefit of the EEC law on free movement. Reg. 1612/68, Art. 1 applies to EEC nationals, irrespective of their place of residence.

12 Art. 227(1)(4). By a Protocol annexed to the Treaty, the Netherlands was permitted to ratify only in respect of its European territory and Netherlands New Guinea.

13 Art. 227(2), Council Decision 68/359. The overseas departments are French Guiana, Guadaloupe, Martinique and Réunion.

14 Art. 135. A list of overseas countries and territories is contained in Annex IV.

15 Art. 227(1)(4)(c) as amended by Art. 26 of the Treaty of Accession.

16 Arts. 52 and 59, on the other hand, specifically limit the right of establishment and the freedom to supply services to nationals of Member States.

17 Art. 135. Dutch citizens from Surinam and Antilles were added to the list of those falling within this Article in 1962. For a discussion of the problem see, Edens and Patijn (1972) 9 C.M.L.Rev. 322; Böhning (1973) 10 C.M.L.Rev. 81.

18 Reg. 1612/68, Art. 1. But its legality depends upon the correct interpretation of Art. 48 which, since it is directly applicable, confers rights upon individuals enforceable in national courts.

19 Treaty of Accession, Protocol No. 3, Art. 2 and 6. But their rights in the U.K. are expressly preserved.

20 Treaty of Accession, Art. 133, Annex V.

21 On the other hand, the interpretation of the term "worker," for the purpose of the Treaty, is a matter of Community law which will not necessarily coincide with national law: *Vaassen Gobbels* [1966] C.M.L.R. 508.

22 *Internationale Handelsgesellschaft mbH* [1972] 1 C.M.L.R. 255, 283.

23 *Nold* v. *European Commission* [1974] E.C.R. 491, 507.

24 *Supra* at p.33. The U.K. Government has not ratified the protocol conferring the right of an individual to enter the state of which he is a national.

25 Note also that the association agreements so far made with African and Caribbean countries do not provide for the free movement of workers.

26 As U.K. and Colonies citizens who have resided here for five years or who acquired their citizenship by registration in the U.K.

27 For workers, see Dir. 68/360, Art. 3; for the self-employed, see Dir. 64/221.

28 Arts. 48(3), 56(1); the grounds for refusal are co-ordinated in Dir. 64/221.

29 Dir. 68/360, Art. 3, Dir. 64/220, Art. 6. Again, these rights are subject to the grounds of public policy specified in Dir. 64/221; if this provision is directly applicable, it gives a statutory base to entitlement to a passport in British law. But the practical change may not be remarkable.

30 *Unger* [1964] C.M.L.R. 319; *City of Wiesbaden* v. *Barulli* [1968] C.M.L.R. 239 (an "idle lay-about" is not a worker).

31 Art. 48(3).

32 See Reg. 1612/68. Art. 10; the spouse and children also have the right to work (*ibid.* Art. 11). The admission of other dependent relatives living with the worker is also to be encouraged.

33 H.C.81, paras.49-54.

34 s.3(2); see also European Communities Act 1972, s.2(2).

35. See *European Commission* v. *French Republic* [1974] E.C.R. 359. (France held in default because a statute discriminated against foreigners contrary to Community law, even though oral directions were given by national authorities not to use the statute against EEC nationals.)

36 See, for example, *Van Duyn* (*supra*).

37 s.2(1)(4). See *Van Duyn* [1974] 1 W.L.R. 1107.

38 Dir. 68/360, Art. 4, Dir. 64/220, Art. 3.

39 Reg. 1612/68, Art. 10(3). This represents a compromise between the views of the Commission and Italy, on the one hand, and Germany and Holland on the other, which have housing shortages.

40 Dir. 68/360, Arts. 4, 6; Dir. 64/220, Art. 3.

41 Dir. 68/360, Art. 7.

42 See Reg. 1251/70.

43 See also Art. 48(3)(d).

44 H.C.82, paras.32-39.

45 *Ibid* para.34. But once the permit has been issued it may not be revoked simply because the worker is unemployed.

46 This is a requirement under the general rules relating to the admission of families (see paras.33, 34), but it is unclear whether it is intended to extend to Part V which deals with EEC nationals.

47 Cmnd. 5715-5718.

48 Arts. 7, 48(2), 52, 59, Reg. 1612/68, Art. 7.

49 The House of Lords in *London Borough of Ealing* v. *Race Relations Board* [1972] A.C. 342 held that discrimination on the ground of current nationality did not fail within the term "national origins" in the 1968 Race Relations Act. In the 1975 White Paper, *Racial Discrimination* (Cmnd. 6234) proposed including nationality as a prohibited ground of discrimination. See also *Cumings* v. *Birkenhead Corporation* [1972] Ch.12; *Edwards* v. *SOGAT* [1971] Ch.354.

50 Arts. 48, 52 and 59 are directly applicable; *Van Duyn* [1974] C.M.L.R.I., *Walrave and Koch*, Case 36/74.

51 *European Commission* v. *French Republic* [1974] E.C.R. 359. Although immigration rules are not technically delegated legislation, they do have the requisite characteristics of publication and formality to satisfy the European Court's requirements.

52 s.2(4); for example, restrictions upon the employment of aliens in merchant ships and their holding pilotage certificates are contained in the Aliens Restriction (Amendment) Act 1919, ss.4, 5.

53 s.8(6).

54 s.7(1)(2).

55 s.8(10).

56 *Supra*, n.48, especially Reg. 1612/68, Titles I, II.

57 [1973] C.M.L.R. 501.

58 [1975] C.M.L.R. 262.

59 Case 33/74.

60 The right to work in another Member State is subject to the requirements of that state's law; Reg. 1612/68, Art. 1, Arts. 52 and 59 of the Treaty of Rome.

61 Case 36/74.

62 Arts. 48(4), 55.

63 Thus Reg. 1612/68, Art. 8 excludes from the right to belong to a trade union, participation in or membership of bodies governed by public law. This might include, for example, N.E.D.C.

64 See Aliens Employment Act 1955, s.1(1)(2). Employment in the armed forces is probably within the exception; see Army Act 1955, s.21(1).

65 *Reyners* v. *Belgian State* [1974] C.M.L.R. 305.

66 Reg. 1612/68, Art. 3.

67 Art. 49; Reg. 1612/68, Parts II and III.

68 For example, Reg. 1612/68, Art. 16 allows offers to be made personally to non-Community nationals by name when the job requires specialist qualifications or there are family ties between the employer and the worker. The Regulation does not jeopardise a Member State's continuing to allow preferential immigration rights to people from non-European countries in a special relation with the Member State (Art. 42).

69 Reg. 1612/68, Art. 20. See also the Joint Declaration in the Treaty of Accession.

70 Art. 48(3), 56(1).

71 Dir. 64/221.

72 Ibid. Art. 4, and Annex. It is unlawful to deport an EEC national on health grounds if the condition arises after the first residence permit has been issued.

73 Ibid. Art. 2(2).

74 Ibid. Art. 3.

75 [1974] C.M.L.R. 1

76 [1974] 3 All E.R. 178.

77 *Supra* notes, 22, 23.

78 Case 67/74. *Cf. Lee* [1975] Imm. A.R. 75 (H.C.80 para.4 does not justify refusing an extension to an over-stayer simply to discourage others).

79 Penncuick V.-C. thought "the plaintiff's view is well arguable; indeed, I think it might be put a good deal higher than that".

80 The contrary view was taken by a German court in *Re Prohibition of an Italian National* [1971] C.M.L.R. 540, and by a Dutch court in *Diederions and Plaschke* v. *Dutch State* [1973] C.M.L.R. 509.

81 A deportation order can be challenged before the appellate authorities on the ground that it is not in accordance with the law; this, by virtue of the European Communities Act 1972, s.2, should include EEC legislation. Persons refused entry normally have no right of appeal before leaving the U.K. But in *Van Duyn* no objection was made to the plaintiff's applying directly to the High Court without leaving the U.K. Contrast *R.* v. *Peterkin ex p. Soni* [1972] Imm.A.R. 253.

82 See 1971 Act s.30 which provides for the removal of mental patients.

Chapter 6

DEPORTATION AND OTHER FORMS OF REMOVAL[1]

There is little necessary connection between deportation and immigration policy, although legal powers to deport have been appended to legislation designed primarily to regulate immigration. The immigration rules identify categories of people who will be admitted and are based on considerations of broad policy in areas such as employment, housing and race relations. Deportation decisions, on the other hand, are more commonly made in the light of the particular circumstances of individual cases,[2] although important issues of general policy do sometimes arise, *e.g.* political asylum and the objectives that may legitimately be pursued via deportation.

Since immunity from deportation is the natural corollary of freedom from immigration control rather than a right to enter or remain in the United Kingdom, it is not surprising to find that their scopes coincide,[3] subject to the recent Prevention of Terrorism (Temporary Provisions) Act 1974. Because deportation decisions are largely individualised and the reliance interest is of less importance than in immigration, the published rules relating to deportation do not give much guidance as to how discretion will be exercised in a given case. They do no more than set out some of the factors that the Home Secretary considers in reaching decisions.

The "interest" in not being deported has been recognised by the courts and by legislation as generally ranking higher than the "interest" in being admitted. For deportation may derogate from an initial decision to admit, may have a disastrous impact upon the way of life of the individual and his family and may carry a serious moral stigma. Much the same may, however, be said of the individual who is refused entry because he is personally unacceptable although he satisfied the general criteria for admission.

An obvious reason why legislation controlling immigration has included a power to remove is that removal may be the most effective way of enforcing the controls on entry.

Who may be Deported

Subject to the exceptional cases discussed below, any non-patrial is liable to deportation even though he has indefinite leave to remain in the United Kingdom; in theory this includes a non-patrial citizen of the United Kingdom and Colonies with no other citizenship. Such people have been removed from the United Kingdom on being refused entry.[4] But the ensuing international opprobrium has been a source of embarrassment to the British Government.[5] The Prevention of Terrorism (Temporary Provisions) Act 1974 confers powers upon the Secretary of State to exclude persons suspected of terrorism; the scope of the powers is not limited by reference to patriality.

Prior to the Immigration Act 1971 Commonwealth citizens, British protected persons and citizens of Eire could only be deported by the Home Secretary on much narrower grounds than aliens.[6] Moreover, ordinary residence in the United Kingdom for the previous five years conferred total immunity from deportation. This coincided with the time at which a right to claim citizenship of the United Kingdom and Colonies accrued. Commonwealth citizens under the age of 17 were immune from deportation.

As part of its policy of assimilating the position under immigration law of all subject to its controls, the 1971 Act extended the scope of the existing powers to deport aliens to all non-patrials,[7] subject to the existing immunities of Commonwealth and Irish citizens.[8] Thus, Commonwealth and Irish citizens ordinarily resident in the United Kingdom on January 1, 1973 are immune from deportation on the ground that their presence is not conducive to the public good if they have since been continuously resident in the United Kingdom and Islands. They are also immune if they have ordinarily been resident in the United Kingdom and Islands for the five years before a decision to deport on any ground; for deportation following a court recommendation the five year period runs from the date of conviction. However, the "family deportation" power is extended to Commonwealth citizens ordinardily resident when the 1971 Act came into force, although this ground was not previously available against Commonwealth citizens.

A person may be "ordinarily resident" for the purpose of claiming these exemptions even though he has remained in the United Kingdom in breach of the immigration laws[9]: those who entered illegally, however, presumably fall within the scope of the *Azam* decision. Thus a Commonwealth citizen who entered clandestinely after March 12 1968 and who remains in the United Kingdom may be deported under the 1971 Act on a ground not previously available to the Home Secretary.[10] Similarly, such a person can never qualify for the five year immunity. Although the amnesty announced by the Home Secretary, Mr. Jenkins, in April 1974 in favour of those who entered clandestinely before January 1, 1973 appears only to apply to the exercise of the power to remove, it is submitted that it should extend to illegal entrants claiming the benefit of section 7. For the amnesty's rationale was the desirability of preserving immunities of existing residents from the retroactive elements of the 1971 Act.[11] The abolition of the immunity from deportation after five years' residence for Commonwealth citizens entering after

January 1, 1973 is linked to the abolition of their right to citizenship based on residence in the United Kingdom.[12]

Whilst the provision of legislative justice for transitional cases is always purchased at the expense of simplicity, it is unfortunate that the immunities from exclusion under the Prevention of Terrorism Act 1974 depend upon different periods of time. For the Act exempts citizens of the United Kingdom and Colonies from removal from Great Britain if they are and have been for the last 20 years ordinarily resident in Great Britain or were born in and throughout their life have ordinarily been resident in Great Britain.[13] Whilst this is not technically deportation because it does not involve removal from the United Kingdom, it is a remarkable interference by Government with the liberty of the individual to live where he chooses.[14] It might also expose a person ordinarily resident in the United Kingdom to liability to internment without trial in Northern Ireland.[15] The 1974 Act was modelled on an earlier Act of 1939[16] and its relationship with the Immigration Act appears not to have been considered.

Exclusion orders may be made against persons who are not citizens of the United Kingdom and Colonies — whether aliens or Commonwealth citizens (even though patrial) — preventing them from entering or remaining in the United Kingdom, without regard to the length of their period of residence here. Potential anomalies are not difficult to imagine: the man born in Belfast who has been ordinarily resident in Great Britain for 21 years is immune; the naturalised or registered citizen of the United Kingdom and Colonies who has been so resident for only 19 years is not.[17] If it is considered as part of a body of legislation empowering the Executive to impinge upon individuals' freedom of movement, the 1974 Act is significant in that it treats aliens and Commonwealth citizens alike and confers immunity upon citizens of the United Kingdom and Colonies by reference to their connection with Great Britain.

Grounds of Deportation

Given the concept of the nation-state it is not difficult to argue for the state's power to deport "undesirables" who do not "belong" to it. The problems, however, lie in formulating acceptable definitions of the key concepts. As we have seen, for historical reasons British law for immigration and deportation purposes defines "belongers" in a complex manner that only partially coincides with citizenship of the United Kingdom and Colonies. Whilst the persons to whom the deportation power applies is largely governed by legal rules,[18] the circumstances in which such persons may be deported are left largely to the discretion of the Home Secretary, subject in some cases to a right of appeal to tribunals independent of the Executive.

When Parliament made its first modern attempt in the Aliens Act 1905 to define the grounds upon which aliens could be deported, it limited them, broadly speaking to criminal conviction and destitution[19]. The Secretary of State's power was only exercisable after an initial judicial determination adverse to the alien and was subject to appeal to an administrative tribunal. Since the Aliens Restriction Act 1914, however, Parliament has effectively left the definition of "undesirable" aliens to the discretion of the Secretary of State, by empowering the Secretary of State to deport when he deems the individual's deportation conducive to the public good.[20] Whilst a power of this width is understandable in the context of the war-time conditions in which the 1914 Act was passed, it is regrettable that the statutory discretion has not been subsequently effectively limited. Indeed, the 1971 Act has extended it to all non-patrials. The problem, of course, is that it is difficult to identify in advance all the circumstances in which deportation may be desirable Parliament has identified some of them, *e.g.* convictions, breach of immigration control, the deportation of a head-of-household and national security. It has also stated that these are not exhaustive. It is regrettable that after more than 50 years' experience of the exercise of deportation powers, it was not found possible in 1971 to define in the legislation much more precisely the circumstances in which the Executive could so drastically interfere with individual liberty.

Few would argue that there are not circumstances in which a criminal conviction justifies a state in deporting the offender, although the principles upon which the power is exercised may be controversial. Should deportation be a substitute for imprisonment? On what grounds is it justifiable to treat a ''non-belonger'' more harshly than a ''belonger,'' by imposing the same penalty and deporting — especially when deportation may have more grave consequences for him and his family than temporary imprisonment? Is the state only justified in deporting a convicted person when there is ground to believe that he may commit offences in the future? By what criteria are offences that should be punishable by deportation identified? How are the individual's length of residence in the United Kingdom, his employment record, his family ties, to be weighed?[21] It is perhaps not surprising that no very clear answers emerge either from the courts making the recommendations or from the Home Office.[22]

The table below illustrates that many court recommendations are not implemented, not, apparently, because Home Secretaries think that they should decide each case *de novo*,[23] but because many leave voluntarily, or under supervised departure[24] or new facts are brought to the attention of the Home Secretary that were not before the court.

Similarly, the desirability of a power to deport for breach of a condition attached to a limited leave to enter or remain in the United Kingdom[26] is difficult to deny, although the way in which the power is exercised will turn to an extent on the gravity with which such breaches are viewed. Again, the immigration rules give no clear guide to Government policy;

Grounds of Deportation 103

they state that a person who has "persistently contravened or failed to comply" with the law will "normally" be deported; "full account is to be taken of all relevant circumstances." [27] The existence of a right of appeal against deportation orders on this ground[28] goes some way to ensure consistency in administrative decision-making, by way of fact-finding based on judicial procedure, interpretation of the terms of the paragraph (*e.g.* persistent contravention) and weighing the personal circumstances of the individual. But

Table

	Irish	Commonwealth	Alien
1963	253 : 152	214 : 105	91 : 40
1964	233 : 140	182 : 93	93 : 38
1965	243 : 161	150 : 95	99 : 45
1966	316 : 171	140 : 82	113 : 47
1967	287 : 183	111 : 72	133 : 66
1968	293 : 177	184 : 100	182 : 87
1969	239 : 142	279 : 233	246 : 121
1970	178 : 142	315 : 233	302 : 121
1971	174 : 116	361 : 225	289 : 127
1972	151 : 122	338 : 237	320 : 123
1973	91 : 58	304 : 223	282 : 142
1974	79 : 45	189 : 113	370 : 126
As average per cent deported/ recommendations	63 per cent.	65 per cent.	43 per cent.

Note to Table

.The first figure in each column is the number of court recommendations and the second, the number of deportation orders made.(25)

the Tribunal regards itself as bound by the statement in the rules of Government policy that deportation normally follows such breaches of conditions.[29]

A new ground of deportation specifically set out in the 1971 Act is that an individual is the wife or child under 18 of a person against whom a deportation order has been made.[30] This was a new head only in the sense that it was not previously specifically contained in legislation; but deportation on this ground had been effected on the conducive to the public good ground under the Aliens Orders.[31] But its inclusion in the Bill provoked a storm of protest, *inter alia*, on the grounds that it imposed guilt by association, that it was sexually discriminatory presuming that women were incapable of supporting themselves independently of their husbands and that it might have disastrous effects upon children largely brought up in the United Kingdom. The force of these arguments was partially recognised by a detailed listing in the immigration rules of the factors that the Home Secretary would consider before exercising his power. Moreover, the rules state that it will normally be appropriate to deport neither a wife who is settled in her own right or who has been living apart from her husband, nor a child who has left home and is working and is independent.[32] The narrowing of the operation of the family deportation clause following its publication as a specific objective of government policy vividly illustrates the merit of substituting a more openly and clearly articulated policy and standards limiting the exercise of power for virtually unbridled discretion.

Whilst there has been little controversy over the legitimacy of the objectives implied in the existence of a power to deport criminals and to enforce immigration law, the exercise of the residual power of the Home Secretary to deport when he deems it conducive to the public good raises fundamental questions of the uses to which the power may be put:

particularly since the courts play a minimal role here in regulating the power of the Executive over individual liberty. The issue of principle transcends the small numbers involved.[33] But it should be remembered that similar grounds exist for the refusal of entry and of renewal of leave for those otherwise qualified within the rules.[34] The exercise of this power raises similar problems, except, of, course, that to require a person to leave the United Kingdom within the period of his leave defeats the expectation created by the original exercise of discretion in his favour. As a matter of fact, however, deportation does not necessarily cause more hardship to the individual and his family than refusal of entry or of a variation of his leave to remain in the United Kingdom.

Neither the law nor Ministerial statements provide very clear guidance about the policy objectives to be pursued through deportation on residual grounds. The Act itself mentions national security, diplomatic relations and reasons of a political character.[35] Not that these are free from ambiguity: distinguishing between protecting legitimate public interest and suppressing political ideas and their lawful expression is difficult for the conscientious and liberal Home Secretary. The handling of the *Dutschke* case caused concern in this respect.[36] During the Committee Stage of the 1971 Act, the Home Secretary, Mr. Maudling, stated that whilst it was not the practice to deport people because of their political views deportation was justified to remove persons of extreme political views who might make speeches that would be found highly offensive by a section of the public or whose presence would give widespread offence.[37]

On the few occasions when an attempt has been made to challenge the removal of a person on non-conducive grounds, the courts have recognised the width of the Home Secretary's legal powers whilst maintaining that in theory the power is not unlimited.

(a)   *Substantive limitations*

It is clear that the courts could set aside a deportation order made against a person statutorily immune from deportation; the existence of the cause, not the status of the individual, is committed to the Home Secretary's discretion. Some possible legal limitations on the cause have been canvassed before the courts.

(i)   *Disguised extradition.* The principal issue raised in *R. v. Brixton Prison Governor ex p. Soblen*[38] was whether it was lawful to deport on the public good ground a person whose return had been requested by the country of which he was a citizen where he was wanted to stand trial or to serve a term of imprisonment following a conviction. Dr. Soblen, a citizen of the United States, had been convicted of espionage there; he jumped bail pending an appeal and fled to Israel. The Israeli Government put him on a plane bound for New York in the custody of a United States marshal. The plane was due to land in London for refuelling and the United States Government had requested the United Kingdom Government to refuse him leave to land. The Home Secretary was prepared so to do. Soblen, however, whilst still in flight, cut his wrists and he was admitted to a London hospital for medical attention. He was served with a notice of refusal to land and a deportation order; his plea for political asylum was rejected by the Home Secretary.

On the application for *habeas corpus* it was argued that this was disguised extradition; the Extradition Act 1870 did not apply to espionage. The request of the United States Government for Soblen's return and the refusal of the British Government to allow him to board a plane for Czechoslovakia — which was willing to receive him — were used to show that the Home Secretary had used his power to deport to achieve another purpose, *viz.* extradition of a fugitive criminal. The Court of Appeal unanimously refused the application: they rejected the argument that the Home Secretary had acted *ultra vires* simply because the effect of the deportation order on Soblen would be the same as if he had been extradited. Nor did they accept that the existence of the request excluded the possibility of deportation. The test was the purpose of the Home Secretary. If he made the order because he thought it conducive to the public good, then it was lawful.

The Court recognised the difficulty of proving the Home Secretary's purpose, particularly when, as here, he claimed Crown privilege for the communication between the American and British authorities. But they were prepared to accept that if a prima facie case of unlawfulness could be raised by the applicant, then the court could draw an inference adverse to the Home Secretary from his refusal to give an adequate explanation of his reasons.

The Court held that no such prima facie case had been estblished, although they gave different reasons for their conclusion. Donovan L.J. said that the notion of public good enabled the Home Secretary to deport to a friendly power one of its citizens convicted of espionage on behalf of a common potential enemy. Pearson L.J. agreed with this and referring to the Home Secretary's refusal to allow Soblen to go to Czechoslovakia said that the notion of public good included "the international consequences of him going east or west." Both agreed that in the unlikely situation of the Home Secretary being shown to have deported solely to comply with a request and not because he thought it for the public good to accede to the request, the deportation order would be invalid.

Lord Denning, however, based his judgment on a narrower ground[39]: he thought that the relevant public good upon which the Home Secretary might well have relied was the undesirability of allowing Soblen to evade the previous decision to refuse him leave to land. He appeared to regard the exercise of that power as unreviewable because before their admission to the United Kingdom aliens had no interests that the courts could protect.[40] Lord Denning is careful, however, to define deportation as removal of a person from the United Kingdom to the country of which he is a citizen.

Subject to this last point, once it is conceded that it is permissible for the Home Secretary to consider the international implications of refusing to return a person wanted in connection with criminal proceedings abroad, then the overlap between deportation and extradition is substantial.[41] The 1971 Act makes the matter even clearer, both by referring to diplomatic relations as a head of public good and by conferring a power upon the Home Secretary to name the country to which the deportee is to be removed.[42]

(ii)   *Political refugees*. Whilst the law leaves to the Home Secretary's discretion the extent to which he balances the public good against individual liberty, the Immigration Rules provide that a person will not be deported "if the only country to which he can be removed is one to which he is unwilling to go owing to well-founded fear of being persecuted for reasons of race, religion, nationality, membership of a particular group or political opinion."[43] This is the first legislative appearance of such a provision in British immigration law since the Aliens Act 1905 excluded political refugees from the class of undesirable aliens who could be refused entry.[44]

Given the historical contexts in which the 1914 and 1919 Acts were passed it is not surprising that they contained no similar provisions. Thus in *Soblen*, although it is unlikely that he would qualify under the current immigration rules for political asylum, the Court of Appeal stated that decisions on political asylum were non-justiciable. It is regrettable that when immigration law was overhauled in the 1971 Act the Government was not prepared to provide specifically in the Act for political refugees.

To what extent the courts now have power to set aside a

deportation order on the ground that it does not comply with the Immigration Rules' provision for political asylum is unclear. It should be noted that the Rules are framed as a statement of Government intention as to the way in which discretion will be exercised, and not in a normative manner. The issue arose obliquely in *Ali* v. *Immigration Appeal Tribunal*[45] when the appellant argued that the Home Secretary could not deport him to a country from which he was a political refugee. The Court of Appeal held that on an appeal against the directions for removal contained in a deportation order,[46] the Immigration Appeal Tribunal had no jurisdiction to reverse the Home Secretary's decision, on the ground that the individual was a political refugee, when he was unable to show that any other country would admit him.[47] The judgment of Lord Denning M.R. may suggest that the issue of political asylum is always non-justiciable.

It should be remembered, however, that under the Extradition Act 1870, the courts are entrusted with deciding whether an individual's return is requested for an offence of a political character and that it has been suggested that the courts should give the same meaning to "political" as it has in "political asylum."[48] It is submitted that there is nothing inherently non-justiciable about the concept of political asylum and that the courts should not be deterred by the ambivalence of the wording from intervening to protect individual liberty in accordance with the well established principles adopted by successive British governments.[49]

(iii) *Discouraging activities in the United Kingdom*. Whilst the decision to deport directly affects the individual against whom the decision is made, it may also adversely affect others who are immune from the power. The effect of the deportation of a man upon his wife and children — who may themselves not be deportable — is obvious; these are factors taken into account in making an order. But what if the deportation order is made in order to curtail some lawful activity in which non-deportables are engaged?

In *Schmidt* v. *Secretary of State for Home Affairs*[50] the appellants had been refused an extension of their leave to stay in the United Kingdom as students at the College of Scientology. The Home Secretary's letter made it clear that his decision followed a previously announced policy of withdrawing recognition from the College as an educational establishment for the purpose of admitting as students those subject to immigration control, in an attempt to stop the spread of an organisation, which though lawful in the United Kingdom, was regarded by the Government as socially harmful. The Court of Appeal struck out a challenge to the validity of the decision as disclosing no reasonable cause of action. Lord Denning, M.R. held that the Home Secretary could refuse to extend a leave "for any purpose which he considers to be for the public good"[51]; it was clear from his letter that the Home Secretary thought that the activities of Scientologists were harmful. Widgery L.J., however, equated a decision not to extend a leave with an initial refusal of entry; in neither case does the individual have a legal interest capable of being impinged. Dissenting, Russell L.J. thought it at least arguable that "the written reasons given by the Minister indicate a purpose of discouraging the institute at East Grinstead by cutting off its students rather than a purpose of keeping students away lest they do harm."[52]

Although Widgery L.J. said that "very different considerations may apply to the making of a deportation order"[53] it is unlikely that any court would hold invalid a deportation order made on the grounds advanced in *Schmidt*, for the power is not limited to a consideration of the personal attributes of the individual but is exercisable when the *deportation* is deemed conducive to the public good. Nonetheless, the use of Immigration Act powers to suppress the free, lawful expression of ideas has disturbing implications for civil liberties.[54] Similar considerations apply to the deportation of trade union activists.

(b) *Procedural limitations*

Here, too, judicial intervention has been confined to admonitary dicta. In both *Soblen* and *Schmidt* Lord Denning M.R. stated that no-one could be deported within the period for which he was given leave to remain without being accorded at least an opportunity to make representations.[55] The legitimate expectation that the individual will be allowed to stay for the period of his leave is strong enough to attract judicial protection, despite the width of the substantive power to revoke it. The existence of a statutory right of appeal to an administrative tribunal against many decisions to deport strengthens the argument for procedural fairness at the level of the original decision.

In *Schmidt* Lord Denning M.R. accepted that a decision of the Home Secretary could be set aside on the ground that he had fettered his discretion, although he could quite properly lay down a general policy, so long as he was ready to listen to reasons why, in an exceptional case, that policy should not be applied. And yet Lord Denning denied the appellants' claim that they had a right to make representations before the Home Secretary decided their application. It is important to note that under the Immigration Act 1971, power to deport or vary a leave is vested in the Home Secretary, whereas the decision on entry is vested in the immigration officer. The Act itself can be read as expressly requiring officers to decide according to the immigration rules.[56] There is no equivalent provision that would justify the Home Secretary's deporting or refusing an extension simply by reference to an immigration rule, and refusing to consider any reasonable argument that the individual might make for not applying the rule to him or for attacking the rule itself.[56A]

Removal and Deportation

Illegal entrants[57] and others refused entry can be removed without a deportation order.[58] The decision may be made by an immigration officer, whilst deportation orders are personally considered by a Minister; there are very limited rights of appeal.[59] Illegal entrants may be deported or simply removed. The power to remove without a deportation order does not extend to a person who entered legally but who is in breach of a condition attached to his leave. This limitation recognises an interest in the individual more deserving of protection than that of the person who was never given leave to enter at all or who initially evaded or disobeyed immigration controls. Nonetheless, it is submitted that the safeguards of the deportation procedure should be afforded to illegal entrants who have acquired a *de facto* interest in remaining in the United Kingdom by having started to put down roots. There is no time limitation on the exercise of the power to remove an illegal entrant, but prosecution must be instituted within three years.[60]

The hardships caused by this summary power of removal became particularly apparent after the *Azam*[61] decision, aggravated, of course, by the retroactive operation of the Act. The policy of the then Conservative Government was that such illegal immigrants would normally be removed although the length of residence, employment record and family ties in the United Kingdom were factors that might justify exceptions to the general policy.[62] In 1974, the Labour Home Secretary, Mr. Jenkins, reversed this policy and granted an amnesty from removal to Commonwealth and Pakistani citizens who clandestinely entered before January 1, 1973 and who on that date were immune from prosecution and deportation for illegal entry.[63] Those within the amnesty would be given indefinite leave to remain in the United Kingdom and their wives and children would be allowed to join them on obtaining entry certificates. The amnesty does not render the individual's previous residence in the United Kingdom legal, for example for the purpose of the immunities from deportation under section 7.[64]

The amnesty, however, was expressed to apply only to those who were affected by the retroactive operation of the 1971 Act: it did not apply, for example, to those liable for prosecution on January 1, 1973 for illegally entering since April 28, 1971 who could be deported following a court recommendation,[65] or to those who entered legally but then overstayed, or to those who had entered in breach of a deportation order or after refusal of leave to enter.[66]

Leaving Voluntarily

Unless the provision in the 1971 Act enabling the Home Secretary to contribute towards the expenses of non-patrials and their families who voluntarily leave the United Kingdom to take up permanent residence abroad[67] was intended to be a significant feature of Government immigration policy — which was always denied — the inclusion of an essentially social security matter showed gross insensitivity to the state of race relations in Britain at the time. For it raised widespread fears amongst immigrant communities of forced repatriation, or of its possible use by public officials to harass immigrants, or as the thin end of an alarming wedge.

In operation the scheme has proved unexceptionable: in March 1973 families with a weekly income generally no more than £5 above the supplementary benefit level became eligible for assistance under it. By the end of 1974, 141 applications had been accepted and 491 individuals left the United Kingdom[68]: this is in addition to the average of 100 families per year who are repatriated at public expense under the Supplementary Benefits Commission's scheme. Both schemes are quite different from the 1971 Act's provision for the "supervised departure" of those liable to be deported.[69]

Notes

1.   The position of EEC nationals is discussed in Chap.4.

2   The relevant immigration rules simply state the problem: decisions will be taken on the merits of each case, but this will also be "consistent and fair as between one person and another". H.C.80, para.38.

3   s.3(5), "A person who is not patrial shall be liable to deportation..."

4   For example, in 1972, 76 United Kingdom passport holders who had been refused entry were detained in Italy and France: H.L. Vol. 333, July 19, 1972, c.761.

5   In 1974, an unpublished report by the European Commission of Human Rights found the British Government in breach of the Convention in refusing to admit Asians from East Africa who were United Kingdom passport holders with no other citizenship. The matter was sent to the Committee of Ministers and not the European Court of Human Rights. *The Times*, May 29, 1974, June 5, 1974.

6   Under the 1962 Act (ss.6, 7) the Home Secretary could only deport following a recommendation by a court on a conviction for an offence punishable by imprisonment. For this purpose an absolute discharge counted as a conviction: *R. v. Akan* [1973] 1 Q.B. 491. The Immigration Appeals Act 1969, s.16 empowered the Home Secretary to deport on his own initiative for breach of landing conditions. It was not unknown, however, before 1962 for courts to impose a suspended sentence or a binding over order conditioned upon the accused's 'voluntarily' leaving the U.K. But see *R. v. East Grinstead Justices ex p. Doeve* [1969] 1 Q.B. 136 (justices had no power under Aliens Order 1953 to require accused to enter into recognisance to leave U.K.)

7   s.3(5). The Pakistan Act 1973, Sched. 3, para.1, continues the exception for Pakistani citizens provided that they apply for registration on U.K. and Colonies citizens before September 1, 1974.

8   s.7.

9   s.7(2). This exemption was stated to have been included in order to preserve the previous immunity from deportation, even though a breach of a condition was a continuing offence. In *Re Abdul Manan* [1971] 2 All A.R. 1016 the Court of Appeal held that a person liable to prosecution for illegal entry could not be ordinarily resident for the purpose of the 1962 Act s.2(2)(a).

10   Although there is no relevant authority on the point, the legislation prior to the 1971 Act did not expressly require that the residence be lawful.

11   At most, the terms of the amnesty appear to turn unlawful residence into lawful residence at the time that the immigration position is regularised by the Home Secretary. The question is whether such regularisation should be given retrospective effect.

12 1971 Act, Sched. I, amending the British Nationality Act, 1948.

13 s.3(4). An exclusion order was revoked when it became clear that the individual would have been resident in Great Britain for 20 years if a few months' service on an English-registered merchant ship was included: *The Times*, January 22, 1975. Of 15 people excluded from Great Britain, 10 had resided there for more than five years: of 10 people excluded from the United Kingdom, 7 had been resident for more than five years: H.C.885, February 6, 1975, c.615 (written answers).

14 It was the Government's intention normally to prosecute terrorists, but to use the powers under the Act when the evidence received was of a "sensitive nature" and could not be used in court. This presumably means where the only evidence is supplied by informers. By November, notices of the making of exclusion orders had been served on 72 people: H.C. 901, November 26, 1975, c.885.

15 See Northern Ireland (Emergency Provisions) Act 1973, Sched.I. As of November 1975, 38 persons were removed to Northern Ireland; some were detained by the police on their arrival, but later released: H.C. Deb.Vol.901, Nov. 26, 1975, c.886.

16 Prevention of Violence (Temporary Provisions) Act 1939.

17 s.3(2), however, does require the Home Secretary to have regard to whether the person ordinarily resident has a connection with any territory outside Great Britain that makes it appropriate to remove him.

18 However, acquisition of citizenship of the United Kingdom and Colonies by virtue of naturalisation or registration is (subject to transitional provisions for Commonwealth citizens already resident in the United Kingdom on January 1, 1973) largely within the Home Secretary's discretion. He also has a discretion to deprive a person of patrial status by revoking a naturalisation or registration. (B.N.A. 1948, s.20.)

19 s.3.

20 1971 Act s.3(5)(*b*) is the successor to the Aliens Order 1953, Art. 20(2)(b).

21 See Statement of Immigration Rules for Control After Entry, H.C.80, para.40, H.C.82, para.47.

22 For a more detailed discussion see D.A. Thomas, *The Principles of Sentencing*, Chap. 6 and F.O. Shyllon, (1971) 34 M.L.R. 135.

23 When Mr. Maudling was Home Secretary he stated that he would only refuse to implement a court's recommendation for very strong reasons (H.C. Deb.Vol.889, January 27, 1972, c.1608).

24 s.6(6) authorises the Secretary of State to contribute to the travel costs of persons who have been recommended by a court for deportation, and his family. H.C.82, para.47 states that this is particularly suitable for young or first offenders, but that they will be prohibited from re-entry. The practical result is, therefore, virtually the same as deportation.

25 Whilst the number of recommendations made for each class is similar,

there is a markedly lower actual deportation rate for aliens.

26 1971 Act s.3(5)(*a*). It was routine Home Office practice to give to an applicant for a variation of status leave to remain pending a decision: *Enorzah* [1975] Imm.A.R.10. The practice was later discontinued to prevent "abuse" of the system of over-stayers: *Islam* [1975] Imm.A.R.106.

27 H.C.80, para.40, H.C.82, para.42.

28 1971 Act s.15(1)(*a*).

29 See *e.g. Dervish* [1972] Imm.A.R. 48; *Derrick* [1972] Imm.A.R. 109; *Jordan* [1972] Imm.A.R.201.

30 ss.3(5)(*c*), 5(3)(4).

31 *R.* v. *Home Secretary ex p. Bressler* (1924) 131 L.T. 386.

32 H.C.80, paras.45-48, H.C.82, paras.52-55.

33 For example, between 1966-70 only six of the 62 aliens deported under this power had not been convicted of a criminal offence in this country: H.C. Deb.Vol.814, March 23, 1971, c.102.

34 H.C.79, para.63, H.C.80, para.65. The power is not exercisable against the wife or child under 18 of a person settled in the United Kingdom, although, of course, they may subsequently be deported on this ground unless within 1971 Act s.7.

35 There is no appeal against the making of a deportation order when the decision was taken on one of these grounds: s.15(3).

36 See Hepple (1971) 45 M.L.R. 501. In January 1975 a deportation order was made on national security grounds against a person, allegedly a member of an Italian Marxist group. He was an active trade unionist in this country: *The Times*, January 4, 23, 1975, *Sunday Times*, January 12, 1975. The order was subsequently revoked before the bearing: *The Times*, January 25, 1975. Aliens promoting industrial unrest in an industry in which they have not been employed for two years are liable to criminal prosecution: Aliens Restriction (Amendment) Act 1919, s.3(2).

37 H.C. Official Report, Standing Committee B, May 20, 1971, c.1162.

38 [1963] 2 Q.B. 243.

39 Donovan and Pearson L.JJ. also agreed on this point.

40 Although Lord Denning does not say so expressly, it would presumably not have been open to Soblen to challenge the refusal of leave to land on the ground that it was made to comply with the request of the United States Government. See also Widgery L.J. in *Schmidt* v. *Secretary of State for Home Affairs* [1969] 2 Chap. 149.

In 1972 two Moroccan Air Force officers were refused leave to enter Gibraltar, after attempting to assassinate King Hassan. They were returned to Morocco, at least partly as a result of a request by the Moroccan Government, without being allowed to make representations or find another country that would admit them. They were then executed and the British Government made an *ex gratia* payment to the widow of one of them after the European Commission on Human Rights had held her claim admissible: *The Times*, August 14, 1974.

41 See O'Higgins (1964) 27 M.L.R. 521.

42 Sched. 3, para. 1(1) empowers the Home Secretary to name the country to which the deportee is to be removed: under the previous law, the only power was to name the vessel or aircraft on which the deportee was to leave.

43 H.C.80, para.50, H.C.82, 57. The Rules also state that when a person is a refugee full account will be taken of the provisions of the relevant international agreements to which the United Kingdom is a party.

44 s.1(3).

45 [1973] Imm.A.R. 33.

46 There was no right of appeal to the tribunal against the decision to deport because it was made on the recommendation of a court. See also *Fardy* [1972] Imm.A.R. 192.

47 See H.C. para.54, H.C.82, para.61 which make this quite clear.

48 *Schtraks* v. *Government of Israel* [1964] A.C. 556, 591.

49 Similar issues have recently arisen on the refusal to admit Chileans who claimed political asylum. The Government refused to grant political asylum to deserters from the United States' Army who objected on conscientious grounds to fighting in Vietnam: they were handed over to United States' military authorities in this country, whether they deserted here or abroad, under the Visiting Forces Act 1952, s.13, apparently without the possibility of judicial review.

50 [1969] 2 Ch. 149.

51 *Ibid*. at p.153.

52 *Ibid*. at p.155.

53 *Ibid*. at p.156.

54 See the Report into the practice and effects of Scientology by Sir John Foster (1971) arguing that it is wrong to refuse Scientologists the normal visitors' leave of three months but acceptable to refuse to admit them as students of Scientology, thus denying them the 12 months' leave to remain normally granted to students.

55 Thus narrowing the scope of *R.* v. *Leman Street Police Station Inspector ex p. Venicoff* [1920] 3 K.B. 72. The hearing might be limited to the determination of the primary facts, rather than the policy merits.

56 Sched.2, para.1(3). "In the exercise of their functions under this Act immigration officers shall act in accordance with such instructions (not inconsistent with the immigration rules) as may be given to them by the Secretary of State." *Cf. R.* v. *Chiswick Police Station Superintendent ex p. Sackstedter* [1918] 1 K.B. 578, 586, 591.

56a In *Enorzah* [1975] Imm.A.R.15, the Tribunal held that the Home Secretary could refuse to entertain an application for an extension of leave if "repetitious.".

57 This includes those who enter without leave or in breach of a deportation order: s.33(1). In 1973, 172 illegal entrants were removed and in 1974, 139:

H.C.892, May 22, 1975, c.540-546. (written answers).

58 Sched. 2, paras.8-10.

59 s.16. The argument being that the illegal immigrant should not be in a better position than the person removed on refusal of entry: the latter, however, generally has a right of appeal from abroad: s.13(3).

60 s.28. This applies to those who entered after April 28, 1971, otherwise it is six months. See *Waddington* v. *Miah* [1974] 2 All E.R. 377. Remaining in breach of a condition is not a continuing offence: *Singh* v. *R*. [1974] 1 All E.R. 26.

61 [1973] 2 All E.R. 765. Many of those removed who were immune before the 1971 Act came into effect had lived in the U.K. for more than three years: H.L. 341., April 12, 1973, c.888. Others had been interviewed by the police and subsequently released because the six months' limitation on prosecution had expired: H.L.343, June 29, 1973, c.1244.

62 However, each case was considered personally by a Minister.

63 H.C.Deb.Vol.872 April 11, 1974, c.637-638: those who had already been removed were allowed to re-enter on obtaining entry clearance: H.C.872, May 3, 1974, c.573 (written answers). By 1975, 1,107 applications for the Jenkins amnesty had been granted.

64 In *Birdi* v. *Secretary of State for Home Affairs*, (1975) 119 S.J. 322, the Court of Appeal held that an applicant for the amnesty had no rights capable of infringement by denial of procedural fairness. However, the Home Secretary said that a Minister would personally consider every deportation and removal order made against a person claiming benefit of the amnesty: H.C. Deb.Vol.888, March 11, 1975, c.104-105 (written answers).

65 The new three years' limitation period is applicable: s.28.

66 1962 Act ss.4(1) and 11(1) made these continuing offences.

67 s.29: the Secretary of State is required to see that expenses are only paid when departure is in the best interests of the individual and that he wishes to leave.

68 H.C.885, January 21, 1975, c.377 (written answers). The average cost per family was £654: H.C.888, March 12, 1975, c.151 (written answers). The scheme is administered through the International Social Services organisation.

69 s.5(6) applies to those liable for deportation under s.3(5)(c) or (6): they are generally not allowed to re-enter (H.C.82, para.47: no equivalent provision for Commonwealth citizens). See also the powers of removal under the Mental Health Act 1959, s.90 as amended by the 1971 Act, s.30

Chapter 7

THE REVIEW OF DECISIONS

From the introduction of the Aliens Restriction Act 1914 until the Immigration Appeals Act 1969 came into force there were no statutory rights of appeal from immigration or deportation decisions. The provisions in the Aliens Act 1905[1] for appeals to tribunals were swept away in the war-time emergency legislation of 1914.

Between 1914 and 1969 there were, however, some opportunities for reviewing decisions of the Executive. But they mostly rested on administrative "concessions," not law and fell far short of a system of appeals. For example, in 1919 an advisory committee was established to recommend to the Home Secretary exemptions from the exercise of the power to deport former enemy aliens. The Home Secretary continued to refer certain deportation orders to a committee but the system effectively ended in 1939 when the committee refused to support the proposed deportation of an alien who had entered by bribing an immigration officer. From 1956 an opportunity to be heard before the Chief Metropolitan Magistrate was given to aliens who had been resident here for the prior two years against deportation orders made on grounds other than a recommendation of a court following conviction, or national security. An appeal to a higher court against a court's recommendation for deportation lay as against sentence. In 1968 an advisory committee was established to consider the withdrawal of passport facilities and exclusion from the United Kingdom of persons normally resident in Rhodesia.[2] Since 1967 complaints of maladministration in the making of some immigration and passport decisions have been considered by the Parliamentary Commissioner for Administration. None of these administrative reviews bound the Home Secretary. Lastly, the supervisory jurisdiction of the High Court was an ultimate check upon the illegal exercise of immigration powers, although given the width of these powers, this could be only a peripheral form of review.

A number of reasons can be found for the absence of any effective review machinery in an area where the individual's interests in freedom of movement, family unity and personal security — all normally highly protected by legal safeguards — may be catastrophically adversely affected. First, the 1919 Act, annually renewed for more than 50 years, was originally regarded as "experimental."[3] Secondly, an alien's freedom to enter or remain in the United Kingdom was not generally regarded as a "right" that should be infringed only after judicial process. This attitude can also be seen in the reluctance of the courts to subject governmental decisions adversely affecting "privileges" to the same standards of procedural fairness as they applied, for example, to the infringement of property interests.[4] However, the new climate created by the House of Lords in *Ridge* v. *Baldwin* spread, to a limited degree, to immigration decisions affecting a right or "legitimate expectation" of the individual.[5] Thirdly, the importance of discretion, rather than of clearly defined rules, in the Minister's decisions was regarded as inimical to close judicial scrutiny, particularly on a subject with a strong prerogative flavour in which "reasons of state" were not infrequently likely to feature.

The 1969 Act reforms stemmed from the changed climate of thought about administrative law and the extension of immigration controls in 1962 and 1968. The general desirability of statutory appeals to administrative tribunals had become, since the Franks Report, part of the accepted wisdom about the appropriate machinery for resolving disputes between the individual and the state. Tribunals had become widely used to review government decisions when the focus of the dispute was the individual's entitlement to the receipt or continued enjoyment of a statutory benefit. The classification of the interest as "right" or a "privilege" did not determine whether a statutory right of appeal to an independent tribunal was appropriate. In response to a demand for more open decision-making the Home Office published the instructions issued to immigration officers which regulated their exercise of statutory discretion. It was clearly more appropriate for tribunals to review the application of these rules than to substitute in all cases their discretion for that of the Minister or the official.

The Wilson Committee's Report stated: "However well-administered the present law may be, it is fundamentally wrong and inconsistent with the rule of law that power to take decisions affecting a man's whole future should be vested in officers of the executive, from whose findings there is no appeal."[6] A more sceptical view of the utility of appeal tribunals was expressed by Mr. Maudling when, as Home Secretary, he was piloting the 1971 Act through the House of Commons: "I have never seen the sense of administrative law in our country, because it is only someone else taking the Government's decision for them. I cannot see that [tribunals] are better qualified if it is not a legal but a practical matter."[7]

Changes in the substantive law of immigration also contributed to a recognition of the need for more judicial scrutiny, in particular the extension of immigration law to Commonwealth citizens, including some United Kingdom passport holders. Certain aspects of the 1962 and 1968 legislation made more pressing the requirement of fair administration, including the right of appeal. For example, the principal justification of the 1962 and 1968 Acts was that they were required to promote harmonious race relations. Unless the administration of the legislation could be seen to accord with the standards of justice normally accepted for resolving disputes between the state and the individual, race relations were likely to be damaged by the suspicions of unfairness harboured by immigrants, particularly from the new Commonwealth. Secondly, the terms of the legislation raised more justiciable issues than the aliens legislation. For example, the right of entry given to returning residents and to the wife and children under 16 of Commonwealth citizens resident in the United Kingdom raised issues of statutory interpretation and factual questions that could be suitably resolved by judicial process. Thirdly, the legislation both restricted common law rights and created statutory rights in respect of the free movement of British subjects. The elements of discretion and privilege that permeated the aliens legislation were less pervasive in the control of Commonwealth immigration. Finally, the Home Office may have seen an appeal system as relieving it from some of the political pressure that has surrounded immigration law and its application since the 1962 Act.

The Right to Appeal

The appeal provisions in the 1971 Act largely continue the system established by the 1969 Act; they apply irrespective of the citizenship of the individual. In examining the scheme of this part of the Act two factors should be considered; first, the value placed upon the individual's interest affected by the original decision, and secondly, the suitability for tribunal determination of the issues raised. The 1905 Act retained to the Secretary of State the application of such key statutory terms as "immigrant ship," "immigrant" and "offence of a political character."[8] An evaluation of the Act's provisions must in large part depend upon one's view of the proper place of legal methods and machinery in reviewing the administration. It is always relevant to ask whether any likely improvement in the quality of decisions subject to appeal will outweigh the administrative costs in manpower, of delay and money. Even though an appeal may not be justifiable when viewed against this type of short term costing, it may be required by the longer term consideration that commonly held notions of fairness demand it. For the effectiveness of a legislative programme — particularly in this sensitive area involving individual liberty and strong public opinion — will be damaged if its administration is regarded as unfair.

(i)   *Decisions from which no appeal lies*
      The fixing of criteria for the issue of work permits is not subject to judicial review. For this is a legislative function depending on governmental assessments of the demand for particular types of labour, the desirability of forcing an industry to increase its proportion of capital investment to labour costs, raising wages or recruiting and training resident labour, and the wider implications of increasing the population through immigration. The application of the criteria to individual cases also involves judgments based upon technical considerations (*e.g.* job classification)[9] and on facts not normally established by judicial procedures (*e.g.* housing and educational resources available and the social consequences of increasing the local immigrant community). However, whether a person qualifies as a businessman, self-employed person or a student rather than as an employee for whom a work permit is necessary is reviewable on appeal.[10]
      Moreover, the interest of the employer-applicant in increasing his labour force by the issue of a work permit is not regarded as of such importance as to justify the benefit of a right of appeal. However, it can be argued that the position is

different when the Department of Employment decides not to renew a work permit after a year.[11] For here the question is whether the interest of the individual in obtaining a variation of his status once in the United Kingdom — which is normally subject to appeal — outweighs the tribunal's relative lack of expertise.

Passports are still issued by virtue of the prerogative. Although a passport — or equivalent document — is a virtual necessity for international travel, it is doubtful whether anyone has a legal right to a passport[12]; there is no right of appeal against a refusal.[13] The strength of the interest in freedom of movement surely justifies a right to judicial review. The refusal or withdrawal by the Foreign and Commonwealth Office of passport facilities from citizens of the United Kingdom and Colonies is by no means rare.[14] The Government has published rules that regulate its exercise of discretion.[15] Justiciable issues of fact and discretion may be raised by a denial of passport facilities for failure to repay the expenses of repatriating a holidaymaker stranded abroad or to a minor allegedly proposing to leave the country against the wishes of his parent, guardian or a court order. Despite the possible reluctance of the authorities to disclose the evidence or the precise grounds upon which they rely, the importance of the interests in personal freedom involved also justifies an appeal against a denial of passport facilities on the ground of public interest.[16]

Other important decisions from which there is no statutory right of appeal include refusals to admit to citizenship, and to issue special vouchers to United Kingdom passport holders subject to immigration control.[17] Patrials refused entry because they did not have a required certificate have no right of appeal against the decision that they require leave to enter.[18] The Divisional Court has also held that a refusal to admit such a person is unreviewable by *certiorari*.[19]

(ii)   *No appeal if decision made on specified grounds*

No appeal lies against decisions adversely affecting a person's claim to enter the United Kingdom if the Secretary of State is of the view that exclusion is conducive to the public good.[20] An appeal against a decision that affects a person's right to remain in the United Kingdom lies unless the Secretary of State is of the view that exclusion is conducive to the public good in the interests of national security, diplomatic relations or for reasons of a political nature.[21]

The reason why an appeal can be brought by a person already in the United Kingdom against a decision made on a ground that would have deprived a person not in the United Kingdom of an appeal, is the greater value placed upon the interest in remaining than in entering. By assimilating the appeal rights of a subject of a deportation order and those of a person refused an extension of his stay, the 1971 Act has been more generous than the courts in determining procedural rights.[22] The expectation of admission aroused in a person to whom an entry clearance or work permit has been issued is recognised by his being allowed to appeal whilst still in the United Kingdom.[23] But because the legalistic distinction between interests in remaining and entering may not in individual cases in fact represent greater and lesser degrees of hardship, the right to appeal should only ever be excluded on the narrower grounds applicable to decisions affecting the interest in remaining.

The reason for excluding an appeal on the specified heads of public policy (i.e. national security and diplomatic interests or political reasons) is that the issues are "non-justiciable." For the Executive, as the politically responsible branch of government occupying a unique position to evaluate the demands of national security and foreign policy, should retain ultimate control of the decision. Although cases in which decisions made for these purposes are rare, the result of any one case may be important in itself.[24] Secondly, to require the Executive to disclose its supporting evidence is inherently likely to imperil the sources of intelligence. The alternative premise is that the state should not use immigration law to protect these interests.

The 1969 Act tackled this problem by providing a "special" tribunal procedure for national security cases.[25] This machinery was used only once, in the case of *Dutschke*; the element relevant to this discussion that caused such dissatisfaction was that in certain aspects of its procedure, *e.g.* the appellant's right to legal representation, the tribunal had a strong judicial flavour. However, neither the appellant nor his legal adviser was fully informed of the case against him, and had no opportunity to cross-examine the witnesses testifying against him on "sensitive" matters. This evidence was not included in the tribunal's opinion, which consequently did not reveal the precise grounds of decision. Moreover, the tribunal's recommendation was not binding upon the Secretary of State. In short, the tribunal's procedure gave a misleading appearance of being judicial in nature.[26]

The 1971 Act abolished the statutory right of appeal against a deportation order made on security or diplomatic grounds or for a reason of a political nature. The addition of this last category might well be thought an inappropriate reduction in the role of judicial check upon the exercise of Executive discretion on an important matter of individual liberty. Instead, a non-statutory hearing is available to those who have no right of appeal because the decision was made on the ground of public good. Representations may be made to three advisers under a procedure similar to that used when a civil servant is disciplined for breach of security. The hearing will be oral, but without legal representation. The individual will be told as much of the case against him as will not compromise the government's source of informaion. The advisers' recommendations will be made in confidence and will not bind the Home Secretary.[27]

Deportation decisions made on the recommendation of a court remain outside the tribunals' jurisdiction,]28] although Wilson argued that it would aid consistency and distinguish deportation from punishment if an appeal lay to the tribunals.

(iii) *Decisions from which a restricted right of appeal lies*

The numerically most important category is the appeal at which the appellant has no right to be present. Although he may be represented at the hearing, the appellant's success may largely depend upon the effectiveness of his friends and relatives in the United Kingdom. Refusals of entry clearance or of entry when the passenger has no entry clearance or work permit are the principal decisions from which an appeal may be made only whilst the appellant is outside the United Kingdom.[29] Appeals against refusals to revoke deportation orders are also in this category.[30]

The common feature of these decisions is that they all relate to persons who do not at the time of decision have leave to enter or remain.[31] It is arguable that persons refused entry certificates because they have not satisfied the official of the factual basis of their entitlement should be allowed a full right of appeal. For the entry certificate is essentially only a method of proving a legal right.[32] On the other hand, because of the numbers and the travel distance involved, these are also the decisions in respect of which the administrative difficulties of temporary admission to attend the hearing are greatest.

In an appeal where it is alleged that an official document upon which the appellant relies is a forgery and that it would be contrary to the public interest to disclose the method of detection, the tribunal must direct that part of the evidence be heard in the absence of the appellant and his advisers.[33] This would, of course, be regarded as intolerable in criminal proceedings where the liberty of the individual from being imprisoned is at stake. But an unfavourable decision in an immigration appeal may be just as serious to the individual. When the appellant is legally represented, the evidence should be disclosed to the lawyer; in other cases the appellate authorities should have a discretion on the procedure appropriate to the particular case.

A person served with notice of an exclusion order under the Prevention of Terrorism (Temporary Provisions) Act 1974 may make representations to the Home Secretary who must refer them to the advisers that he has appointed for this purpose unless "he considers the grounds to be frivolous." [34] For most practical purposes this qualification places the right to make representations before the advisers within the Home Secretary's discretion. Legal representation before the advisers will be allowed, but there will be no opportunity of knowing or meeting the evidence supporting the Home Secretary's view of involvement in terrorism. It should be recalled that this last term is loosely defined as "the use of violence for political ends."[35] The justification offered for the retention of final power of decision in the Executive is that national security may be at stake. So it may be. But as long as the normal processes of the criminal trial are regarded as adequate to protect this interest for the vast majority of people in this country, is it justifiable to deny them to persons regarded both by nationality and immigration law, and by the laws conferring civic rights, as full members of the community?

The right of appeal against removal as an illegal entrant is limited to the validity of the directions for removal[36]; the right is normally only exercisable after the individual has left the United Kingdom.[37] The illegal entrant is thus worse off than the person refused entry, even though he may have resided in the United Kingdom undetected for a considerable time. Apart from the special provisions under which seamen or members of a crew may be admitted temporarily to join a ship or aircraft,[38] a person who has been given leave to enter must be dealt with by the deportation procedure. This reflects a legislative desire to punish and deter the "queue jumper" and recognises the interest acquired through an initial lawful entry, even though a breach of the conditions of the leave to remain renders the residence unlawful.[39]

(iv) *Full right of appeal*

After taking into account the "exceptional" circumstances described above, the decisions against which a full right of appeal is available — in accordance with a procedure similar to that of many administrative tribunals — are those affecting a person's freedom to remain in the United Kingdom where the original entry was lawful, and a refusal to admit a person with an entry clearance. The destination contained in the directions for removal given to implement the principal decision can also be challenged on appeal.[40]

Curiously, this latter right is not restricted by the ground upon which the principal decision was made. Thus if Dr. Soblen had been served with a deportation order under the 1971 Act he could have appealed against being removed to the United States even though he could not appeal against the making of the deportation order. Although this may reflect the Home Office view that the Government's interest in deportation proceedings is limited to removal from the United Kingdom, the destination specified in the order might raise issues regarded elsewhere in the Act as non-justiciable. Whether Dr. Soblen should have been permitted to go to Czechoslovakia, a country willing (and eager) to receive him and to which it would have been cheaper to send him,[41] was clearly a highly political issue.

An appellant usually has a two-tier appeal, first to an adjudicator and then, with leave, to the Immigration Appeal Tribunal.[42] But from decisions against the making of a deportation order on the grounds of conducive to the public good or as a member of a family of a deportee, appeal lies at the first instance to the Tribunal, presumably because the issues likely to be raised are less "justiciable."[43] Conversely, there is an automatic right of appeal from the adjudicator where an appellate authority is satisfied that at the time that the immigration officer decided that the passenger required leave to enter or leave was refused the appellant had a certificate of patriality or an entry clearance.[44]

Jurisdiction

The appellate authorities may reverse a decision from which an appeal lies if satisfied that the decision was not in accordance with the Act or the immigration rules or, when made in the exercise of a discretion, that the discretion should have been exercised differently.[45] It is important to note that the rules only partially ensure equality in the Executive's administration of policy, for the Secretary of State is free to waive the rules in favour of an individual; the exercise of this dispensing power is not reviewable by the tribunals.[46]

An appeal on the ground of non-compliance with the Act or rules will be allowed if the appellant satisfies the tribunal that the decision was wrong in fact or law. When the appeal is against an exercise of discretion, the tribunal's jurisdiction is to "apply [its] mind to the problem afresh and to determine what in [its] judgment was the correct exercise of discretion."[47] Thus the tribunal may review *de novo* an exercise of discretion conferred by a rule, even though the decision was in accordance with the rules.

The distinction between rule and discretion lies along a continuum from clear, imperative directions (*e.g.* a passenger seeking admission as a dependant must hold a current entry clearance[48]) to an open discretion (*e.g.* visitors may be allowed to stay as trainees if the Department of Employment considers the offer of training to be satisfactory).[49] But discretion may be limited in other ways. First, the exercise of discretion may be limited by a general statement of policy contained in the rules, for example, that immigration officers will perform their duties without regard to race, colour or religion[50] and that students are expected to leave at the end of their studies.[51] But the tribunals do not regard themselves as bound by Government policies not contained in the rules.[52] Such general principles and examples as are in the rules may influence the view taken by the tribunal of the scope or appropriate exercise of a discretion. For example, in *Costa*[53] the Tribunal considered the discretion to admit a Commonwealth citizen, who had been away too long to return as of right, "for example, if he has lived here for most of his life." The Tribunal deduced from the example that the underlying principle was that a person should not have discretion exercised in his favour unless he could show strong connections with this country through length of residence and family or other ties.

Secondly, the rules may guide the exercise and the tribunals' review of discretion by listing factors to be considered. For example the rules provide that in deciding whether to grant a variation of conditions, consideration should be given not only to the formal requirements but also to whether the individual has observed the conditions upon his original leave and whether his conduct or character makes his remaining undesirable.[54] The rules list personal factors, such as length of residence, family ties, the ability to subsist without recourse to public funds and compassionate circumstances, which will be considered before a person is deported as a member of a deportee's family.[55]

Thirdly, the tribunals' discretion may be restricted by an open-textured standard, as in the previous rule that husbands were to be admitted where it would be undesirable because of the degree of hardship that would be caused if the wife could only live with her husband outside the United Kingdom. The tribunals regard decisions taken in these circumstances as raising issues of compliance with the rules, not the exercise of discretion.

(i)   *Decisions in accordance with the rules*

A decision challenged on the ground that it was not in accordance with the Act or the immigration rules may require the tribunal to undertake different types of inquiry.

First, it may call for an interpretation of the Act or a rule, or of the relationship between more than one arguably applicable rule. The resolution of such issues does not turn primarily upon the particular facts of the individual case but will establish an approach to the application of a provision and will tend to set general guidelines for settling future disputes. Although the rules are drafted in a relatively simple, non-technical form, the tribunals are here exercising traditional judicial skills of discerning the intended meaning of rules from the internal evidence of the instrument, referring both to policies expressly stated and to inferences drawn from analogous provisions in the rules, and respecting any limitations inherent in the words chosen to express the rule-maker's intention.

For example, in *Andronicou*[56] it was held that an entry clearance was not "current" for the purposes of entitling its possessor to appeal against his exclusion whilst still in the United Kingdom, if it had already been used to gain entry, even though it was still valid in that it was being used within six months of issue. Similarly, in *Zaman*, [57] the Tribunal held that a parent could not qualify for admission as being "dependent" upon his child unless *financially* dependent and the payments made were *necessary* to the parent. In *Martin*,[58] the Divisional Court upheld the Tribunal's decision that a person who did not qualify for a variation of a condition under any single category in the rules could not qualify by partly satisfying one rule and partly another.

Secondly, the tribunal's function may be to decide whether a provision applies where the primary facts are agreed and the general meaning of the rule is clear. One case may involve questions of interpretation and application. In *Emmanuel*[59] an appeal was brought against the exclusion of a child on the ground that the parent in the United Kingdom had not had "sole responsibility for his upbringing." The Tribunal held that as a matter of interpretation "sole responsibility" was not to be understood literally but whether the responsibility was "sole" was to be determined by reference to any other person and not only the other parent. Whether on the agreed relevant facts the standard was then satisfied was a question of application.

Thirdly, the tribunal may have to decide whether the primary facts have been established by the evidence. Since so many decisions depend upon findings about an individual's intentions or upon facts not easily proved because of distance and poor public records, the tribunals are often not well placed to settle a conflict of evidence, especially when the appellant is not present. But tribunals have reversed decisions on the basis of fresh evidence or a favourable impression made by the sponsors.[60] The record of the interview made by an entry certificate officer is difficult to rebut. Moreover, in *Padmore*[61] the Tribunal held that, although desirable, it was not obligatory for an immigration officer whose decision was challenged to appear at the hearing to be cross-examined. But one case may raise important questions of interpretation as well as essentially factual disputes. For example, in *Perween Khan*[62] the Divisional Court held that a passenger did not qualify under the 1962 Act on the ground that he wished to enter the United Kingdom for the purpose of attending a course of study, if this was not the primary purpose. "Purpose" included an intention, if leave was subsequently granted, to remain, after the period of study.

Whilst the burden and standard of proof applicable in any

case clearly involves a legal interpretation, whether the evidence in an individual case satisfies the standard may involve legal or factual issues. For example, in *Amrik Singh*[63] the Divisional Court stated that it was not justifiable to infer solely from the passenger's absence of funds that he did not intend a visit, at least where he had relations in the United Kingdom able and willing to support him without his taking employment. Similarly, in *Mohan Singh*[64] it was not justifiable to infer from the fact that a passenger could have obtained medical treatment in his own country that he was not seeking entry for the purpose of medical care. The fact that there were no job opportunities at home for a person with the training for which the applicant was seeking entry could support an inference that he was not genuinely seeking entry as a studey.[65] The relevant issue is whether the student intends to leave the United Kingdom at the end of the period of study, and not whether he will return home. In many of these cases the tribunals are not making *de novo* findings of the fact, but deciding whether the inference drawn by the original decision-maker is, in all the circumstances, including his experience, reasonable.

(ii) *Discretion*

Because the Act empowers the tribunal to substitute its own judgment on the merits of the case for that of the Secretary of State or an official, the tribunal's first task is to decide whether the case before it is governed by a rule or discretion. The tribunal must then decide the scope of discretion allowed by the rules and then, if still relevant, how the discretion should have been exercised.

For example, in *Howard*[66] the Tribunal held that the discretion to admit a child under the age of 18 to join a parent in the United Kingdom "because family or other considerations' make exclusion undesirable", does not extend to considering whether the child would be better off in the

United Kingdom unless the child's circumstances abroad were so "intolerable" as to make exclusion undesirable. Subsequent decisions do not always indicate whether the tribunal is dismissing the appeal because the facts fall outside the scope of the discretion defined by the rules or outside the principles formulated by the tribunal for the review of the exercise of discretion.[67]

A similar problem may arise where a rule prescribes a result on given facts, subject to a discretion illustrated by an example. In *Costa*[68] the rules gave a discretion to admit a passenger who had been away for too long to qualify for entry as of right as a returning resident, "if, for example, he. has lived most of his life here." The Tribunal held that although the example only guided the exercise of discretion, the underlying principle of the provision was to benefit only those with "strong connections with this country by a combination of length of residence and family or other ties". The Tribunal must have regarded these factors as limitations imposed by the rules upon the discretion, for it stated that "We have some sympathy for the appellant ... but it is not our task to take into account compassionate circumstances." [69]

The question raised by these cases is whether the tribunals have not taken too narrow a view of their jurisdiction to review an exercise of discretion on the merits. There are other situations where the existence of a discretion may not be apparent because not expressly conferred by the rules. Neither the Act nor the immigration rules prescribe the procedure to be followed by those making the original decision from which an appeal is made. The courts have, through their supervisory jurisdiction, read certain minimum standards of fairness into the legislation; their observance is a condition precedent to the lawful exercise of the statutory powers. But it is open to the tribunals to decide on the merits whether officials should, as a matter of discretion — even though not mentioned in the rules — adopt standards above those enforced by the courts. For example, in *Padmore*[70] one ground of the appeal was that the officer who decided to exclude the appellant was not the one who had interviewed him. In *Alibhai*[71] the appellant challenged the propriety of the entry certificate officer's discussing the application with a superior officer before deciding. In both cases the Tribunal's primary concern appears to have been whether the procedure complied with the standard established in Re *K.(H.)*. The Tribunal only very briefly considered whether as a matter of discretion additional procedural standards were appropriate. Similarly, the tribunals have limited their consideration of such flexible terms as "hardship" and "sole responsibility" to whether the decision is in accordance with the rules, even though the interpretation and application of these words involves a substantial discretionary element.

The reported decisions do not reveal any general principles underlying the tribunals' review of the exercise of discretion, apart from weighing the public interest (as represented by the Home Office decision) against the compassionate and other factors militating in favour of the individual. Often, of course, it will be difficult to go further than this without the tribunal's unduly limiting its discretion. But in recent years the courts have formulated rules from the general notion of fairness in order to test the legality of administrative decisions.[72] The scope for the tribunals to develop this concept in their appellate jurisdiction for the exercise of discretion is much broader. One aspect of fairness is that like cases should be treated alike; this notion has been deployed by the tribunals in some cases. But it should also be open for an appellant to argue that because a similar case was decided in favour of the individual, he too was entitled to a favourable decision, at least when the rules conferred a discretion.[73] Similarly, an individual might be entitled to a favourable exercise of discretion because he had been materially misinformed by an official, or an earlier decision had been made without any change in the relevant facts.[74] It might also be unfair to apply retrospectively a change in policy.

Critique

The appellate system has not escaped criticism. It has been said that the tribunals, partly because of the background in the colonial service of some of the members, have been too prepared to accept the evidence offered on behalf of the Home Office and too ready to conclude that the appellant or his witnesses are not telling the truth. The tribunals, as has been suggested, have taken too narrow a view of their jurisdiction and have preferred to decide cases by reference to rules of an unduly technical and restrictive nature. The Court of Appeal recently quashed a decision of the Immigration Appeal Tribunal on the ground that it had erred in law by construing too narrowly the "special circumstances" in which it could hear an appeal out of time.[75] The tribunals were adopting a narrower view of the hardship that a wife had to prove before her husband was admitted to live here than the Home Office did in early 1974. It may also be that the price of judicialisation is the reluctance of the Home Office to respond to the intervention of an M.P. or other interested person, and depart from a decision, upheld by a tribunal on appeal.

On the other hand, the tribunals are not bound by Home Office policies that are not expressed in the rules.[76] Thus they could prevent the Home Office from changing the principles upon which a discretion was exercised, for example, whether to vary leave to remain from visitor to student status. The statistics below also show that a significant number of decisions have been reversed on appeal that might otherwise have stood.

Table 1
July 1, 1970 – July 31, 1974: Commonwealth Citizens

Original Decision	Exclusion	Refusal of e.c.	Variation[2] of Conditions	Decision to Deport	Refusal to revoke	Destin-ation	Total
Appeal Decisions[1]	205	7,374	1,245	55	23	77	8,979
Appeal Allowed	28 (13.6 per cent.)	1,695 (23 per cent.)	111 (8.9 per cent.)	8 (14.5 per cent.)	6 (26 per cent.)	3 (4 per cent.)	1,851 (20.5 per cent.)

Notes to Table 1

1. This column excludes appeals lodged that were withdrawn or abandoned and decisions pending.

2. This includes refusals to vary.

Table 2

Appeals to Adjudicators from January 1, 1973 – July 31, 1974 under Immigration Act 1971

Original Decision	Adjudicators' Decisions[1]		Appeals allowed	
	Commonwealth Citizens	Others (excl. EEC nationals)	Commonwealth Citizens	Others (excl. EEC nationals)
Exclusion	131	62	30(23 per cent)	4(6.7 per cent)
Exclusion from Abroad	279	238	9(3 per cent)	12(5 per cent)
Refusal of entry Certificate	1477	68[2]	410(27.7 per cent)	15[2]
Variation of Conditions[3]	639	333	38(6 per cent)	6(1.8 per cent)
Making of Deportation Order	126	3	8(6.3 per cent)	0
Total	2652	704	495(19 per cent)	37(5.2 per cent)

Notes to Table 2

1. This column excludes appeals withdrawn or outside the tribunal's jurisdiction.

2. These figures comprise refusals of visas and Home Office letters of consent.

3. This includes refusals to vary.

One point to emerge from these figures is that the success rate in appeals does not bear any evident relationship to whether the appellant has a right to attend the hearing. Thus the high rates of success are recorded for appeals against refusal of an entry clearance and in Table 1 against refusal to revoke a deportation order. It is, however, true that an appeal is lodged in only about one-fifth of the refusals to grant entry certificates to Commonwealth citizens, but whether these were the strongest cases or those where the appellants had the benefit of active sponsors in the United Kingdom is impossible to tell. The high success rate for appeals made in the United Kingdom against exclusion may suggest that immigration officers are giving insufficient weight to the entry clearance presented by the passenger. The low rate of success in appeals made from abroad against exclusion may be explained on the grounds that passengers who do not obtain entry clearance are probably not qualified to enter or, at least, that the tribunals view with suspicion claims that have not been locally investigated by the entry certificate officer.

The publication of the immigration rules which accompanied the creation of the appeal system has significantly extended the scope of the supervisory jurisdiction of the High Court. For in the cases so far reported, it has been assumed that a decision that conflicts with the immigration rules may be quashed for error of law on the face of the record,[77] although the Court may require the applicant first to exhaust his statutory remedies. It may also be that the limiting of statutory discretion by the rules and the consequent creation in the individual of an expectation that a favourable decision will be made will encourage the courts to extend the same procedural and substantive protections against the abuse of power conferred by immigration law as they have done elsewhere when important interests of the individual are at stake.

Notes

1   s.2. From 1906-13, 7,006 aliens were excluded for want of means; 55 per cent. appealed with a 41 per cent. success rate (or 23 per cent. of all refusals on this ground). 2,409 aliens were excluded for medical reasons; 40 per cent. appealed with a 23 per cent. success rate (or 9 per cent. of all refusals on this ground). The higher rate of success in the former category is largely explained by job offers that materialised before the hearing.

2   H.C.766, June 17, 1968, c.723-724; H.C.767, June 27, 1968, c.126-130 (written answers). The chairman of the committee was Mr. Justice Cairns.

3   The emergency context in which the 1914 Act was passed was seen as still existing in 1919.

4   See, for example, *ex p. Venicoff* [1920] 3 K.B. 72. Similar reasoning was used to deny a right to a hearing before a trader's licence was revoked: *Nakkuda Ali* v. *Jayaratne* [1951] A.C.66.

5   *Soblen* [1963] 2 Q.B. 283; *Schmidt* [1969] 2 Chap. 149; *Re K.(H.)* [1967] 1 All E.R. 226.

6   Cmnd. 3387 (1967) para.84.

7   H.C. Official Report, Standing Committee B, May 25, 1971, c.1508.

8   s.8(4).

9   *Latiff* [1972] Imm.A.R. 76.

10   *Machado* (unreported) TH/2395/71(63). But see *Stillwaggon* [1975] Imm.A.R.132.

11   *Ainooson* [1973] Imm.A.R. 43 (D.o.E.'s decision that the appellant was not an industrial trainee but an employee is not reviewable by the Tribunal).

12   EEC Directive 68/360 Art.2(1) requires member states to grant to EEC nationals the right to leave their territory to seek work within the EEC, "on presentation of a valid identity card or passport" granted "in accordance with their legislative provisions" (Art.2(2)).

13   In 1969 the Government announced that it intended to extend the jurisdiction of the Cairns Committee to include all passport withdrawals: H.C.776, May 25, 1969, c.141 (written answers). But nothing came of this: H.C.881, November 15, 1974, c.265 (written answers). The P.C.A. has jurisdiction in respect of decisions unrelated to national security or criminal proceedings. Dicta in *Att.Gen.* v. *I.B.A. ex rel. McWhirter* [1973] 1 All E.R. 689 suggest the possibility of an extension of the principles of judicial review to the exercise of the prerogative. See too, *R.* v. *Criminal Injuries Compensation Board ex p. Lain* [1967] 2 Q.B. 864.

14   For example, between 1951-68, 2,400 passports were withdrawn, generally for failure to repay repatriation expenses: H.C.764, May 14, 1968, c.110. The numbers are rising.

15 See H.C.881, November 15, 1974, c.265 (written answers): *quaere* whether this limiting of discretion makes easier an argument for imposing a duty to act fairly: see *British Oxygen Co.* v. *Board of Trade* [1971] A.C. 610.

16 Between 1951-68, 20 passports were withheld in the public interest, mostly from suspected mercenaries. The other stated ground for withholding a passport, apprehended evasion of criminal proceedings, could be brought within the ambit of pre-trial criminal procedure.

17 Extra-statutory hearings have been held to consider these latter cases; but the Tribunal has no statutory jurisdiction: *Shah* [1972] Imm.A.R. 56.

18 s.13(3).

19 *R.* v. *Secretary of State for Home Department ex p. Phansopkar, The Times,* April 29, 1975. (s.3(9) requires such persons to prove their patriality for any purpose under the Act by a certificate).

20 s.13(5) (refusal of entry and entry clearance); s.15(4) (refusal to revoke a deportation order).

21 s.14(3) (variations of conditions of leave to remain); s.15(3) (making of deportation orders). Statements issued under the Act setting out the grounds of decisions are conclusive of the person by whom and the ground upon which they were made: s.18(2).

22 *Schmidt* [1969] 2 Ch. 149.

23 s.13(3).

24 In other circumstances, where it is general policy not the individual decision that is important, the Home Secretary can prospectively reverse the appellate authorities by amending the immigration rules.

25 s.9.

26 See Hepple, *Aliens and Administrative Justice: The Dutschke Case* (1971) 34 M.L.R. 501.

27 Following the making of a deportation order in 1974 against an Italian, Caprino, the Government proposed to allow representations to be heard by Sir R. Hayward (a member of the Post Office Board), Sir C. Jarrett (a former civil servant) and Sir D. Hilton (President of the Immigration Appeal Tribunal). Caprino was to be represented by Mrs. M. Dines of U.K.I.A.S. The order was in fact revoked.

28 s.15(1)(*a*).

29 s.13(2)(3).

30 s.15(5).

31 It is not that they are outside the U.K., for a person may have had leave to enter even though there is a deportation order against him.

32 The same argument applies *a fortiori* to those refused or who arrive without a certificate of patriality when required to possess one to qualify to enter as of right. An application for *certiorari* to quash a refusal of entry will not be entertained: *ex p. Phansopkar, supra,* n.19.

33 s.22(3).

34 s.4(4). The first advisers were Lord Alport (a former High Commissioner and deputy Speaker of the House of Lords) and Mr. R. Waterhouse Q.C. (a Crown Court Recorder). Their advice is not binding on the Home Secretary. By late November 1975, 16 out of 64 persons served with exclusion orders had made representations; 5 of the 16 "appellants" were successful.

35 ·S.9(1). In the debate on the new Bill introduced in November 1975, the Home Secretary stated that he would make available to the advisers all the information upon which he had made his order.

36 ss.16(1), 13(4). Illegal entry includes entering without leave and in breach of a deportation order.

37 s.16(2); the exceptional case is where the appellant alleges that he is not the person named in the deportation order.

38 s.16(1)(*b*), Sched.2, paras.12-15.

39 Except for the purposes of s.7.

40 s.17. The right to appeal against directions is broadly brought into line with the restrictions on the right to appeal against refusal of entry whilst still in the U.K. by s.17(5).

41 The Rules direct the tribunal to have "regard to the public interest generally and to any additional expense that may fall on public funds." H.C.80, para.54, H.C.82, para.61.

42 s.20(1). An appellant normally requires the leave of the adjudicator or the Tribunal: Immigration Appeals (Procedure) Rules 1972, S.I. No.1684, rule 14.

43 s.15(7)(8).

44 s.22(5). The rules of procedure provide for an automatic right of appeal when the appeal turns on "an arguable point of law" and when refugee status is claimed: *supra*, rule 14(2).

45 s.19(1).

46 s.19(2) provides that a refusal to waive a rule is not an exercise of discretion for the purposes of s.19(1).

47 *R.*v. *Peterkin ex p. Soni* [1972] Imm.A.R.253, 255, *per* Lord Widgery C.J. In *Dervish* [1972] Imm.A.R.48, the Tribunal appears to have limited itself to asking whether the Secretary of State's decision was wrong.

48 H.C.79, para.40. For conflicting decisions on whether "should" is mandatory, see *Al-Tuwaidji* [1974] Imm.A.R.34, *Vasiljevic* [1975] Imm.A.R. 100.

49 H.C.80, para.16. In *Ainooson* [1973] Imm.A.R. 43 the Tribunal held that when the Department did not approve, then a refusal by the Home Secretary to extend did not present an exercise of discretion for the tribunal to review.

50 H.C.79 and H.C.81, para.2.

51 H.C.80, para.13, H.C.82, para.12.

52 *Howard* [1972] Imm.A.R. 93, 96.

56 [1974] Imm.A.R. 87.

57 [1973] Imm.A.R. 71.

58 [1972] Imm.A.R. 275.

59 [1972] Imm.A.R. 69.

60 *Iqbal Haque* [1974] Imm.A.R. 51. (Tribunal allowed appeal after receiving a report from a physician in London doubting the accuracy of inferences drawn about a child's age by an entry certificate officer from reports that he had seen.) *Afoakwah* [1972] Imm.A.R. 17 (adjudicator satisfied by sponsors that they could support the appellant during her visit to look after the sponsors' children and that she intended to return when the sponsor's wife completed her studies).

61 [1972] Imm.A.R. 1. It would help to require an agreed record of the interview to be signed by the individual and the e.c.o. or immigration officer.

62 [1972] 3 All E.R. 297..

63 [1968] 3 All E.R. 163. See also *Murgai* [1975] Imm.A.R. 86 (non-disclosure of past application for e.c. does not justify finding no intention to leave U.K. after study).

64 [1973] Imm.A.R. 9.

65 *Islam* [1974] Imm.A.R. 83. (The Tribunal held that it was proper for the e.c.o. to consider whether the application was "genuine and realistic" in determining the applicant's primary purpose even though the rule did not contain this requirement.) In *Khan* [1975] Imm.A.R. 26 the Divisional Court held that the 'realism' of the application was irrelevant if the other criterion of the rules were satisfied. But facts germane to "realism" may also relate to "genuineness": *Goffar* [1975] Imm.A.R. 142.

66 [1972] Imm.A.R. 93.

67 See, for example, *Needham* [1973] Imm.A.R. 75; *Ravat* [1974] Imm.A.R. 79.

68 [1974] Imm.A.R. 69.

69 *Ibid.* at p.75.

70 [1972] Imm.A.R. 1.

71 [1972] Imm.A.R. 127.

72 See, *e.g.* the procedural rights stemming from the duty to act fairly (*Re K.(H.)*), the development of estoppel (*e.g. Lever (Finance) Ltd.* v. *Westminster Corporation* [1970] 3 All E.R. 496) and the related decision in *Re Liverpool Taxi Owners' Association* [1972] 2 All E.R. 589.

73 This argument was rejected in *Tosir Khan* [1974] Imm.A.R. 55 but in that case the decision was made under a rule, and the Act specifically prevents the Tribunal from reviewing a refusal to waive a rule.

74 See, Hepple, *supra*, n.26. The tribunal allows the official to justify his decision on a ground different from that stated in the notice, provided that adequate opportunity is given to the appellant to rebut: *Cooray* [1974] Imm.A.R. 38.

75 *Mehta* v. *Secretary of State for the Home Department* [1975] 2 All 1. E.R. 1084: see Immigration Appeal (Procedure) Rules 1972 *supra*, rule 11(4).

76 In 1911 the Home Secretary made a non-binding recommendation to the Board that refugees from political and religious persecution be given the benefit of any doubt about their eligibility for admission.

77 The tribunals are required to give reasons when requested and are within the jurisdiction of the Council on Tribunals: Tribunals and Inquiries Act 1971, Sched.1, para.8. Despite some dicta describing the Immigration Rules as regulations, the 1971 Act only expressly makes them binding vis-à-vis the tribunals. It is doubtful whether a misapplication of this quasi-legislation by an official is reviewable in the courts, except, of course, where it has been upheld by a tribunal.

INDEX